PRAI
THE WOMEN

MW00655186

"In this fast-paced era in which we live, we hasten from one project to the next. We live in a time where instant gratification is paramount; cellular communication disrupts our family time at the dinner table (if we can even pencil in family dinner). Reality television captivates the minds of many. The art of communication has become less and less significant.

In the coalfields of West Virginia, where everybody knew everyone else's name, the family was modeled daily as the most critical institution of which one could ever be a part. Second only to the immediate family were the community ties—in contemporary vernacular—it takes a village to raise a child.

Carolyn Warren reminds us in *The Women at the Table* that the 'village' concept was foundational in preparing her for success. She remembers the voices that molded her from childhood to this day. She introduces us to *the women at the table* (my Aunt Ruth, who raised me, being one of them), who influenced her lifelong journey. Undoubtedly, you will be inspired by their presence in her life and challenged to follow their example to raise up the next generation of women.

So, relax your mind as Carolyn escorts us through time and prompts us to whisper silent thanks to those who impacted our lives. Pull up a chair and be an intentional eavesdropper while carefully listening to *the women at the table*."

—First Lady Serita Jakes, The Potter's House, Dallas, Texas

"When we come to the table with the little we have, we offer someone else something they need. The beauty of kindness is that we don't have to know how to serve others. We just have to be present. Each woman we meet at Carolyn Warren's table is a powerful reminder that extraordinary impact begins with everyday authenticity."

—Nicole Phillips, Host of The Kindness Podcast

"*The Women at the Table* is a phenomenal read! This book is beautifully crafted. Carolyn Warren relates personal experiences and lessons learned throughout her life to build your confidence, resilience, character, and strength. The homages to her mother and other women woven throughout will cause you to appreciate and grow from your own life experiences.

You will find yourself on a self-reflective journey with Carolyn. The transparency of her personal life's reflection is worthy of admiration. Wearing her first pair of heels, discovering her style, suffering the unfortunate death of her father, and witnessing her mother mourn will make an impact on your life. The culmination of life experiences develops us spiritually and emotionally. Tap into the deeper revelation within yourself by reading every page of this book."

—Joy Bivens, Director,
Franklin County Job & Family Services

"*The Women at the Table* is a masterful excavation of time-honored principles that one generation 'cut their teeth on' but another generation seems to have lost. The author graciously brings us back in a way that allows the old to reconnect with the new, ultimately shattering the erroneous ways in which many of us have defined true success.

Get ready to go on a journey of personal discovery as the most ordinary, everyday events make an extraordinary impact on one's life. The women at her table may not be the kind you'd invite to yours.

But they each carry their unique measure and unequivocally show us the power behind having a 'table' at all. Carolyn shows us how our lives are a series of key moments that have shaped and even changed the course of our path.

More importantly, she prods us to intentionally become that architect who creates someone else's key moments—simply by looking for opportunities to pay it forward. She shows us how there is power in finding our end from our beginning and allowing that to become the compass for our future.

The Women at the Table is a celebration of womanhood, motherhood, and sisterhood all at the same time! It transcends gender and race by speaking to the heart of anyone who's ever struggled with purpose, belonging, or understanding to live a life of significance.

I applaud this work and believe it to be a definitive pattern for success, not only for breaking 'old scripts' that have advised us in our past but by inviting us to engage in the process of becoming the very best version of who we were intended to be!"

—Stacy M. Burke, President & CEO, Restorative Financial Services and The ONIONomics Financial Wellness Program

"Carolyn Warren's *The Women at the Table* is a treasure trove of insight, wisdom, and encouragement. She masterfully shares heartwarming stories and painful experiences with the reader, bringing us to the 'table' with her. She wraps each lesson with sincerity and love that provokes the reader to make the most of the unique life experiences that benefit themselves and others.

I would encourage all who read this book to view it as a reference tool for life. *The Women at the Table* is a must-read for those who endeavor to live on purpose and positively impact their communities!"

—Belinda Stockton, Director of Human Resources, Patrick Henry Community College

The *Women* —at the— TABLE

The *Women* —at the— TABLE

Ordinary Women, Ordinary Moments,
Extraordinary Impact

CAROLYN A. WARREN

AUTHOR ACADEMY elite

Published by Author Academy Elite
PO Box 43, Powell, OH 43065
www.AuthorAcademyElite.com

Identifiers:
LCCN: 2020922087
ISBN: Paperback 978-1-64746-593-3
ISBN: Hardback 978-1-64746-594-0
ISBN: E-book 978-1-64746-595-7

Available in paperback, hardback, e-book, and audiobook

"Scripture is taken from the *HOLY BIBLE,
NEW INTERNATION VERSION*

Copyright © 1973, 1978, 1984 International Bible Society. Used by
Permission of Zondervan Bible Publishers."

Any Internet addresses (websites, blogs, etc.) and telephone numbers
in this book are offered as a resource.
They are not intended in any way to be or imply an endorsement by
Author Academy Elite, nor does Author Academy Elite vouch for the
content of these sites and numbers for the life of this book.

To my parents
for giving me the love that every child deserves.
To my husband
for making me smile. You are the love of my life.
To my daughters,
may you continue the legacy of your
mother and grandmother.

To my readers
You were created to make a difference.
Live authentically every day, move beyond your fears,
and model your best life!

CONTENTS

PART FOUR: CONCLUSION— MAXIMIZING THE MOMENT!

FOREWORD

The Women at the Table is more than a glimpse into how to live a successful life. This book shines light on the often unheralded yet life-giving necessity of the people who nurture, shape, and mold us. These people invest their spiritual, intellectual, and physical energies to enable us to live to our highest potential.

In these pages, I hear not only Carolyn Warren's vibrant voice, but I also hear the voices of the marvelous, stout-hearted women who gathered around her mother's table. Their voices are familiar. I hear the voices of *my* mother, grandmother, and next-door neighbor—all of whom were nurtured and mentored by women at *their* table. They are sage women who savored a pitcher of ice-cold lemonade, shelled peas, and snapped beans as they shared the latest news and mentored their own and others' children.

As she shares her story, Carolyn introduces us to women who have played a significant role in her life. Although each woman is unique, they stitch with the common thread of love. Love is given freely and voluptuously as the author is coming of age. Love supports her as she navigates the mercies of walking with grace, forgiving, and learning about the immense power of our beliefs.

Above all, this book is an invitation to remember who and whose you are, an invitation to live your unique genius so you can make the difference in the world that only you can make.

This invitation is a testimony to the transformative power of legacy—not the footprint we leave behind. But the legacy we live, we create each moment of our lives.

**—Gloria J. Burgess, Ph.D., CEO, Jazz Inc.,
Host of Legacy Living Podcast**

INTRODUCTION

MOMENT: a segment of time filled with possibility.

How do we define success? For me, it is marriage for fifty years to the man I fell in love with at nineteen. It means raising three successful daughters, spending a week at a dude ranch in Gunnison, Colorado, and sleeping under the stars in New Mexico.

I've visited the continent of Africa, walked the streets of Jerusalem, and toured the Vatican in Rome. I've had a new house built, stood on the beaches of the Pacific and Atlantic Oceans, served as co-owner of a business, and coached thousands of women.

In society's eyes, I am the definition of success. How I got here, however, is not so simple. In a world that preaches self-reliance and complete independence, My story is entirely the opposite.

Every accomplishment and accolade I have attained is rooted in conversations I overheard as my mother and her friends sat around her kitchen table. The seeds they planted when I was a little girl in the coal camps of West Virginia helped me reach goals and milestones decades later. This book is about the seeds that took root, flourished, and produced fruit.

CAROLYN A. WARREN

I am grateful to those women for transferring their wisdom and life lessons that modeled and shaped my life. Their investment of time and insight, their triumphs, and failures all unknowingly helped me become a productive individual. Each of them created a memorable moment in time when I became the recipient of some gift they possessed, and those gifts empowered me to soar.

What a beautiful thought—that amid our ordinary lives, we can teach what comes naturally to us, affirm someone with an encouraging word, challenge them to move beyond a limiting belief, and paint a picture of a better future. Ordinary people can create extraordinary opportunities for growth in the lives of the people around them.

I believe we can create moments that produce transformation in others and shape their identity. These encounters empower and motivate people to move beyond the status quo and reach goals that were once unattainable. That means we can create windows of opportunity that inspire change!

In this book, you will learn about the needle-movers and the seed-sowers in my life. None of them were famous, wealthy, or college-educated, but each carried something essential for my growth. They transformed my life when they decided to include me in theirs.

Through my life story, you will redefine what it means to live a meaningful life. Each of us must intentionally invest in others and act as catalysts in their development. The women at *my* table knew this principle and practiced it.

CREATE A MOMENT IN TIME FOR SOMEONE ELSE

Some of the stories I share are over sixty years old. Yet, for me, they still carry the spirit of each woman who impacted my life. These women left legacies that continue to teach and guide me. I remember each story vividly because of the impact it had on *my* future.

Join me as I share the stories of the incredible women who prepared me for my successes. As you read, think about the memorable moments you can create every day for others in your life. You, too, might be planting seeds and making an impact, as these women did for me.

IT TAKES A VILLAGE

As a young girl, I remember hearing the voices of the ladies sitting around my mother's kitchen table. As these women spoke, I listened to the rhythm of their distinct voices. At times I heard laughter, excitement, hushed whispers, and even the muffled groans of a heavy heart expressed through what I knew were tears.

They gathered at my mother's house to share the latest news, take advantage of a listening ear, voice their concerns in an environment of acceptance, and sometimes simply to enjoy one another's company.

Their conversation was not intended for my ears because it was "grown folks' talk," but I heard every syllable they uttered. I understood all that was said, and I could infer what was positive or negative by the vocal intonations or the silence that followed each statement. Unknown to the ladies and me, a kinship was being formed—one that went beyond a biological relationship—and helped shape my life.

Eavesdropping on their conversation was easy since my bedroom was near the kitchen. My bedroom was a haven; it was "my space." I craved the quiet of its four walls and would sit and read for hours. This alone time was more enjoyable than playing outside with my friends. My love of solitude caused others to misunderstand me. Adults labeled me "shy," "antisocial," "a loner," or "a bookworm." My playmates assumed I was arrogant when I refused to play with them.

None of these labels were true. I simply thrived in an atmosphere of peace and quiet. Years later, I recognize and celebrate that I am an introvert. I'm one who thrives and energizes with solitude, who prefers listening to talking, and shuns attention. What a revelation! I'm who God created me to be.

WORDS OF WISDOM

Listening to the ladies, I learned practical life skills and insights as valuable as the knowledge learned in a formal classroom. Those lessons prepared me to know what to do during a conflict and take responsibility for my actions. These are some of the simple principles I learned:

The pot can't call the kettle black.
God don't like ugly.
People in glass houses should not throw stones.
The apple doesn't fall far from the tree.
Why would you pay for something that you can get for free?
Definitely don't marry a man who is too lazy to get a job tasting pies in a pie factory (as my mother would often say).

These may sound like clichés without substance, but the truth behind the words taught me how to live successfully. Unknowingly, I developed a systematic way of thinking and viewing the world, which others would later identify as maturity beyond my years.

For me, the kitchen table was more than a place to eat a nourishing Southern meal; it was a storehouse of wisdom and a place of learning. Education is more than memorizing facts or gathering information from the pages of a book. It also encompasses the lives we are fortunate to encounter or experience.

Those seemingly insignificant chance meetings are the keys to unlocking our destiny and equipping ourselves to live on a higher level. Those were the voices that magically replayed in my mind and guided my decision-making when a situation required greater insight.

As mentors, *the women at the table* taught me to be a lady, prioritize the qualities I sought in a husband, rear my children, value a strong work ethic, and be capable and feminine. Wisdom flowed from their lips, and their insights inspired me to live with greater purpose.

MEET THE LADIES

Let me introduce you to the women at *our* table: Mrs. Ruth Martin, Mrs. Eunice Logwood, Mrs. Helen Pennix, Mrs. Janie Scott, and, of course, my mother, Mrs. Mildred Cross—or Miss Millie, as we called her.

Later, Mrs. Ann and Mrs. Jean Roop came, and although they never sat at the table, they both made an immeasurable impression on my life. These are the seven ladies who created a safe harbor and a moment in time for me to grow.

PART ONE
PREPARING FOR SUCCESS

There are critical times in life that are turning points, and they change the trajectory of our lives. These experiences shape us, and we acquire a fresh perspective and new meaning regarding how we view our world.

Life is never the same. Our experiences become building blocks to our future success. These shifts consist of conversations, chance encounters, and even *aha* moments when concepts or new ideas make sense.

These opportunities result in personal transformation. They serve as markers and lift a simple discussion or encounter from ordinary to extraordinary. They function as a key that, when inserted into a lock and slowly turned, unlocks the door to our next phase of growth.

Each step is a time of empowerment that leads us to our destiny and purpose once mastered. Life prepares us to make a difference! Every single day is an opportunity to become a person destined for success.

1

LEARNING BEGINS
WITH A SEED

Education is knowledge that ignites transformation.

Name a person who made an indelible impression on you. Did you name a teacher, a parent, a favorite aunt, a grandparent, or a sibling? That person came to mind because they made you feel special.

We've all met someone who made a profound impact on our lives. That person created a special memory—and became unforgettable. Our encounter was a pivotal moment that signaled a time of change or growth for us, and the relationship became a footnote in our life story. It was a point of reference that authenticated who we are.

For me, that person was Mrs. Ruth Martin. She was tall, stately in stature, wore glasses, and had the smoothest chocolate brown skin I could imagine. She was always appropriately dressed in a simple housedress (the accepted attire for women in the 1950s), and she changed my life. She and her husband, Mr. Goalie, were next-door neighbors and my parents' best friends. My siblings and I respected and viewed them as an aunt and uncle.

During summer, my parents and the Martins bantered with one another on their respective front porches, or "holler," as we say in the country. They enjoyed one another's company. Before telephone service reached our community, they communicated with one another after dark by throwing a small stone at each other's houses. The thump on the side of the house was the signal to go outside and answer our neighbor. In the country, we learn how to be resourceful.

The Martins were surrogate parents to me when my parents were at work. Since Mrs. Ruth did not work outside the home, she became the arbitrator for childhood conflicts between my siblings and me. We trusted her to resolve issues fairly but knew she would inform our mother if we misbehaved. She played many roles in my life, including one I was not expecting.

A TIME OF TRANSITION

I spent my days like every child who did not have a care in the world—playing with my friends. But on my fifth birthday, my life drastically changed. The following year I would start the first grade, and my parents faced a dilemma because there were no preschool or kindergarten in my community for me to attend. How would they prepare me for first grade?

My mother worked outside the home, so they needed a solution. They found a surprising one; it was Mrs. Ruth! The details of that discussion were unknown to me; I was simply informed that she was my new teacher.

My relationship with Mrs. Ruth changed overnight. She was a family friend, a mediator of childhood squabbles, and a source of maternal comfort when my mother was absent—but now she became my teacher. She had a new assignment to prepare me educationally, but more importantly, she became a lifelong supporter and encourager.

Monday through Friday, I was enrolled in Mrs. Ruth's kindergarten class. After lunch, I washed up, put on clean clothes, and, with excitement, skipped through the opening in the fence separating our two properties. This was a special class with a gifted teacher, and I was the only student.

My kindergarten classroom was her kitchen, and my desk the dinner table. Always a gracious host, she offered me a beverage before we started the day's lesson while the room filled with the aroma of the evening meal she was preparing.

MY FIRST TEACHER

The curriculum covered the basics—learning the alphabet and numbers, writing my name and address, and reading. I was acquiring the skills needed to excel in first grade. She was a great teacher, and I was a model student. Each class session was an opportunity to learn and discover something new.

I was fortunate to have a personalized curriculum based on current events, and I could ask all the *why, what,* and *how* questions that came to mind. I gained an excellent foundation for primary school, but more importantly, I learned to read, and I loved it. That skill changed my perspective. It created a world outside the small community I knew. Books became my best friends, and acquiring knowledge was exciting and fun.

Years later, my mother purchased an *Encyclopedia Britannica* set from a traveling salesman, and I cherished each volume. Books permitted me to travel the world, never leaving the four walls of my bedroom; I simply turned pages. When a subject aroused my curiosity, I found a book to answer my questions. Without a doubt, the world was at my fingertips.

Reading became my favorite pastime. It is my hobby— how I prefer to relax and reduce my stress level. A fun day for me is sitting in my favorite chair with a cup of coffee and a book from *The New York Times Best Sellers List.* Books make me laugh, cry, and even smile. Sometimes I will read a paragraph or a page aloud to savor every word fully. Learning information and the pursuit of knowledge are interests vital to my personality.

Several years ago, I took the Gallup Strength Assessment, and one of my top qualities was "learner." That is no surprise to me. I enjoy acquiring knowledge and gaining wisdom through reading.

The time I spent at Mrs. Ruth's kitchen table unlocked a personal strength. Where would I be today if she had said *no?* I would have missed an experience that shaped the rest of my life. When we say *yes* to a need, we become a significant partner in someone's development.

To her little neighbor, she became *Teacher of the Year*—a title that, under normal circumstances, she would not have received. Making an impact may require that we step outside our comfort zone and say *yes* even when we feel unqualified or unprepared.

EDUCATION SHOULD RESULT IN TRANSFORMATION

What is the goal of education? Is it merely a teacher communicating information to a student? Or does it serve a greater purpose? The transfer of facts and theories is essential, but the ultimate goal is to prepare students to impact their community positively. In other words, to teach is to equip the student to take action.

The teacher serves as an initiator, inspiring the student to a moment where growth takes place. If no change occurs, the flow of information between the teacher and student is ineffective or faulty. An alternate learning methodology may be necessary to achieve the desired outcomes.

The Hebrew language provides additional insight to understanding the goal of education. The Hebrew word for *education* is the word *Torah,* and it describes what an instructional encounter between a teacher and a student should accomplish. *Torah* is derived from a root word meaning "to guide" or "to teach" and is defined as "teaching, doctrine, or instruction."

Rebbitzen Denah Weinberg, the Jewish speaker and writer, states, "Torah is not education; it's transformation."[1] Based on Rebbitzen Weinberg's quote, education should be a transformative experience for the student.

The life cycle of a butterfly is an excellent analogy of this process. The butterfly progresses through several stages of growth: the egg, caterpillar, and the chrysalis. Each phase has specific needs and time requirements to develop correctly. When the needs of each stage are met, the butterfly moves to the next phase. But the intermediary steps are not necessarily beautiful and give little indication of the unique characteristics the butterfly will have.

When we see a caterpillar on a leaf or a chrysalis hanging from the twig of a tree, can we identify the butterfly developing within? Most of us cannot. If we only focus on what we see, we fail to recognize the potential that is being processed. But if we allow the metamorphosis to proceed and nurture each stage, ultimately, a beautiful specimen will emerge.

Education is also a metamorphosis. Teachers guide the process and equip their students to become the people they were created to be. A teacher's instruction ensures the student progresses through each stage successfully. Guides are vital partners in their students' learning experiences. Without an instructor, the student's ability to become a person of significance is hindered.

Mrs. Ruth initiated my metamorphosis journey. Her instruction exceeded the transference of information—it revealed who I was and who I could become. My transformation process started with her. An ordinary woman without a college degree became a teacher, a mentor, and a personal development coach. She said *yes* to an ordinary request to help her young neighbor and birthed potential in her. Mrs. Ruth, *"thank you for inviting me to sit at your table."*

"Life isn't a matter of milestones, but of moments."

—Rose Kennedy

TABLE TALK:

What skill, lesson, or principle could you teach to add value to someone?

2

A TEACHER REVEALS
WHAT IS HIDDEN

To teach is to open the eyes, mind, and spirit.

Who was your favorite teacher? We each have at least one name that comes to mind. What qualities inspired you? How did he or she impact your life? Good teachers are role models, influencers, and motivators. They shape the lives of their students by teaching a subject in which they are exceptionally skilled. During the instructional process, a student will develop an awareness of their individual potential.

I was fortunate to have several fabulous teachers, but I have a special appreciation for Mrs. Helen Pennix. She was my Sunday school teacher and neighbor as I grew up. Unlike my middle school teachers at the time, she was not a college graduate, but she had a skill she wanted to share with others. She loved to teach the Bible. In her class, I discovered a passion that would influence my outlook on life.

For many readers of the Bible, the Old Testament is a collection of bedtime stories read to children, having no practical application for real life. For Mrs. Helen, it was different. The Old Testament was a historical record containing keys to overcome adversity. Each story had a purpose: to empower the reader to become a champion. It was the record of super-heroes—not victims.

The message she communicated to her students was; with God's help, anything is possible. And if we followed the examples of those biblical characters, we could also have extraordinary lives.

A TEACHER OPENS OUR EYES

Great teachers are insightful storytellers. They are masters at engaging students and imaginatively presenting vital information. As Mrs. Helen narrated stories from the Old Testament, they became real-life historical dramas in HD. Taking her place in front of the class, notes in hand, she shared the experiences of characters who triumphed over challenges and skillfully defeated their enemies.

There was a message applicable to our lives: be as powerful as the story's hero. An influential communicator, she mentally transported me to the geographical location of Moses as God parted the Red Sea. I observed Abraham preparing to sacrifice his son. From afar, I witnessed David, the shepherd boy, bending down and grasping five smooth stones, then placing them in his bag to take down the giant towering over him.

After the lesson, there was always a lively question-and-answer discussion. Mrs. Helen either had the answer or told us where to look. She inspired us to learn more about the topic as we discussed it.

How was I impacted during these classes? I developed a fascination with historical facts and people. I was intrigued by information but more compelled by the circumstances creating conditions that allowed incidents to occur. Events do not take place in a vacuum; there are always stories behind the stories. According to my Gallup Strength Assessment, this love of history is part of my talent mix, and one of my top talent areas is "context." I enjoy thinking about the past within a contextual theme, and I understand the present by researching history.

Our personal talent mix draws and captivates us because of our intrinsic interest, even when we are unaware of it. Unconsciously, we are attracted to situations where our gift, talent, or skill can be utilized or modeled. That ability joined with our motivation, equips us to become the perfect tool for a future assignment. In other words, our giftedness has a purpose.

My love of history is so ingrained that a historical setting was a prerequisite for years when selecting a

OUR GIFTEDNESS HAS A PURPOSE.

novel to read. It is important to note that this passion was revealed to me in a typical Sunday School class. It was taught by a woman who shared a topic in which she was interested. Sunday after Sunday, I was impacted by her study and preparation. When we develop expertise in a subject, it overflows, and others benefit.

I am a recipient of her surplus. We can learn this life lesson—our ability to impact others may be hidden in the activity, hobby, or skill in which we are proficient but take for granted. We fail to realize that what is second nature to us may change someone's life.

What gift have you acquired that you could intentionally share?

A TEACHER INTRODUCES KNOWLEDGE TO HER STUDENTS

A teacher creates a learning environment that permits an intellectual exchange to occur. Educators must "train up a child (student) in the way he should go, and when he is old, he will not turn from it" (Proverbs 22:6 NIV).

The words "train up" come from the Hebrew word *chanak*, which has four basic meanings. One interpretation defines it as instruction.[2] It means "to introduce someone to something or to someone, to expose them to experiences that will inspire and activate their natural gifts." The introduction process provides guidance and direction to the areas where the student will naturally excel.

This is important because natural gifts or talents often go unnoticed, unrecognized, or taken for granted by the individual. Sometimes it is the acknowledgment or identification by another person that reveals the superpower in our possession.

Sitting in my Sunday School Bible class, I became aware of how my mind organizes thoughts and ideas. I was learning about *me:* my identity and my personality. This love of history shaped my perspective but also prepared me to help others.

Whenever I coach or counsel someone, I often ask, "What were you thinking before you did (or said) that?" "What event or personal circumstance validated *this* decision?" In their response, I seek historical context that helps define their present situation.

With that information, I evaluate their decision-making process and its effect on their current situation. Next, we develop tools and strategies for them to accomplish their goals. Our ability to honestly examine the effectiveness of our patterns of behavior will enhance our capacity for achievement.

This self-development process is called self-leadership, and it is vital to our success. In *The 15 Invaluable Laws of Growth*, John Maxwell says, "If you want to change and grow, then you must know yourself and accept who you are before you can start building."[3] With self-awareness, we can evaluate our skills, talents, and strengths and determine how to leverage them to serve others.

Can you name an ability or secret weapon you carry? An ordinary chance encounter with a person may reveal it to you. Our strengths are tools that increase our ability to connect with others on a deeper level. Do you want to live a life of significance? If the answer is *yes:* Get busy doing what you do well. You might change someone's life.

> *"I am not a teacher, but an awakener."*
>
> —Robert Frost

TABLE TALK:

What individual made you aware of a unique skill you possess? How are you motivated to use that skill?

3

LEARNING TO WALK WITH GRACE—IT DOESN'T COME NATURALLY

Walk is a four-letter word that takes us where we want to go.

A favorite pastime as a young girl was searching for hidden treasures in my mother's jewelry box. Wearing my mother's jewelry, I pretended to be a famous movie star or a beautiful princess attending a ball. Of all the pieces in her box, I prized the earrings because they were easy to put on and instantly transformed my image in the mirror.

My mother had earrings in every color of the rainbow. Some were round, and others dangled from the ear. Some were shiny golds and silvers, and others looked like flowers in a garden. It wasn't easy to decide which pair would be suitable for the imaginary event I was attending with so many options. But selecting earrings was always the first step in getting dressed.

Next, I rummaged through her closet for a pair of heels to complete my make-believe outfit. High heels in every color lined the floor. Which would I choose? Slipping my feet into a pair, I tried to remain upright. Making a selection was the easy part because walking in high heels is a balancing act.

How could I walk while standing on tiptoes in shoes several sizes too big?

I was missing an essential element: I needed time. In time I grew into those shoes and learned to make a graceful entrance to a real event.

WALKING WITH GRACE REQUIRES SKILL

Almost every year at the New York or Paris Fashion Week, a model falls while walking in high heels. It is difficult for professionals to walk in heels, much less a young girl. To prove my point, do a Google search for "models falling on the catwalk" and see how many videos appear.

In fashion jargon, the catwalk is the elevated platform or narrow runway where models parade the latest designer fashions with grace, poise, and skill in five-inch heels. The highest-paid and most in-demand are said to mimic a cat's gracefulness—thus the term *catwalk*.

When I was fourteen years old, I had the opportunity to wear my first pair of high heels on Easter Sunday morning. They were white, two-and-a-half-inch pumps. At my church, it was customary to wear white on Easter. Therefore, I had a dress, shoes, purse, and gloves in white.

My family and I would walk to church, and this was my catwalk. Of course, I needed to prepare for my debut by practicing walking in heels. This skill requires work to attain mastery.

I needed someone to coach me through the process. What better instructor than my mother? At my first lesson, I slipped my feet into my heels and instantly realized I needed instruction. Standing, or more precisely, trying to stand, I became overwhelmed with the thought of falling. But my mother was there to catch me just in case.

I listened as she reminded me to hold my head high and "look straight ahead." She assured me I would *get this* and not fall flat on my face (or worse yet, turn my ankle). Boy, did I need the encouragement! In the back of my mind, I was beginning to question this entire process. *I thought this would be easy. Could I learn to balance my weight on a small, narrow heel? And once I mastered the basics, could I do this with ease?* What else was required? Practice. And more practice.

With hindsight, I realize walking in high heels holds a valuable life lesson. Anything worth doing well requires commitment and repetition. In his book *Outliers,* Malcolm Gladwell summarizes a critical key to success in any field: performing or practicing for ten thousand hours.[4]

Over time, we experience improvement as we work toward achieving any goal. Unfortunately, I did not have ten thousand hours to invest. Besides, the catwalk was not my objective. I only wanted to walk to church and back!

PRACTICE MAKES PERFECT

When someone observes us walking, what does our stride reveal? Does it communicate confidence? Or does it convey the exact opposite? The objective of walking in heels is to display an inner quality through a physical act. Does our stance say, "I like who I am?" Of course, this is not an egotistical mindset but a belief in our self-worth. We are carriers of greatness who contribute to the world and make a difference.

This mindset shift is critical to our success. Can we walk into a room and own it? Can we confidently enter with a self-assurance that conveys, *I belong here.* For a young girl learning to have a presence and the poise to say, *I love who I am,* is the lesson to learn. And it is a hard lesson to master on our own. But our footwear is secondary. It is our poise that exemplifies our inner beauty and self-assurance.

That first pair of heels is our opportunity to learn to be graceful and develop self-confidence. It identifies a life transition—moving from childhood to adulthood. It is a rite of passage that says to the world and specifically to older, wiser women, "I need your reassurance and support to transition properly." Why?

Transitions can be challenging as we enter unknown territory. We are leaving one self-concept with a set of expectations for a new reality that offers more opportunity but requires insight and wisdom. These attributes may not currently be in our toolbox. This lack can result in self-doubt and questioning. The stakes are higher, but it is time to create our own identity and fulfill the ultimate purpose God has for us.

How do we transition through a rite of passage successfully? It helps to have a mother, father, mentor, or coach who is supportive as we go through the process. They transfer their acceptance and blessing during this process, and a deepening of the relationship takes place. They have done it and can provide the insight and knowledge we need.

As I practiced walking in my white pumps, my mother was right beside me, holding my hand as I attempted to find my balance.

She said, "You won't fall."

"You can do this."

"You look beautiful."

Those words of affirmation shifted my thoughts from believing this task was impossible to "Yes, I can do this!" They suppressed thoughts of fear or failure.

Of course, it takes practice and patience to walk in heels with confidence. We must pay attention to the position of our feet. Are they pointing forward? Am I walking in a straight line? If so, we can determine our natural stride and keep moving ahead. These are also the success principles necessary to live life. To be successful, we must master the details, make corrections as needed, and most importantly, keep moving.

Life requires that we focus on a goal and have a vision for our destiny. What do I want to achieve in life? Where do I want to go? As we practice walking in a straight line and managing distractions, we can achieve anything we want.

Stand up straight and focus on your destination. You will find your natural stride and move toward your purpose. Do not give up when you fall. When you feel uncomfortable in shoes that are too big or too high, remember that with practice comes improvement, and success is soon to follow.

WE NEVER WALK ALONE

Rites of passage are initiated when a mentor recognizes that one phase of life is ending and another beginning. With a gentle nudge, they signal that a change is on the horizon. Their wisdom and love guide and shift us into a new reality. We are moving into new territory, but with their assistance, we will make it. They have been where we are going and know the path well.

Easter Sunday finally arrived. As I walked to church in my white heels, I was thankful for the words of affirmation and support from my mother. A lesson on walking in heels became an introductory class about how to live. Life is a continuous balancing act: We are walking through life situations and growing with each experience.

We expedite this process as we extract wisdom and insight from those who have walked the path previously. If we do this properly, we can live with grace. We must continue practicing until we can do it with confidence. But the first step is to start on the inside, let it be the inner beauty that people identify as pleasing. It does not come naturally for most of us, but when we have the support and wisdom of those who love us, there is nothing we cannot accomplish.

"For beautiful eyes, look for the good in others,
for beautiful lips, speak only words of kindness;
and for poise, walk with the knowledge
that you are never alone."

—Audrey Hepburn

TABLE TALK:

Describe a childhood rite of passage. How did that experience shape you as an individual?

4

DEVELOPING A SENSE OF STYLE

Style is an external glimpse of what is on the inside.

D oing anything for the first time makes it memorable. At twelve years old, I took my first vacation, and for me, that was a monumental adventure. I finally left the state of West Virginia to see another part of the country. The longest distance my family had previously traveled was eighty-five miles to Charleston, the state capital, for basketball tournaments. My mom and dad were both avid basketball fans, so basketball season was an exciting time for us. But these were only day trips, never an overnight stay.

The summer of 1963, however, would be different. That summer, I would have a vacation show-and-tell story like my friends. I remember sitting in the back seat of the car and looking out the window, feeling small and anxious, surrounded by adults.

David, my half-brother, was seated in front of me, behind the wheel of his car. In the front passenger seat was his step-father, Mr. Gable, and in the back seat with me was his wife, Lillian, and his mother, Mrs. Sis. David had invited me to spend the summer with his family in Connecticut, and I was thrilled to tag along. It was a little scary, leaving my mom and dad, but I was ready for a real vacation.

As I sat in the back seat, watching cars and trucks roll by and the landscape change, I wondered, *how long will this trip take?* I was curious; *did Bridgeport, Connecticut look like the coalfields of West Virginia? Did the kids play hide-and-seek or Old Maid or softball?* Of course, the big question was, *"Who will I play with?"*

AN UNLIKELY FRIEND

What brings two individuals together to connect and form a relationship? The variables are too many to name, but sometimes they simply click. On the surface, it may be an unimagined match, but for some reason, it works. To my surprise, my new best friend was old enough to be my mother. It was David's mother-in-law, Mrs. Ann.

Upon being introduced, she invited me to visit her home, and we hit it off. It was an odd pairing but one we both enjoyed. Mrs. Ann was stylish, independent, and confident. She radiated a youthfulness I had not observed in an adult woman. My new friend was fun.

Her home was a big two-story house, and she was the sole occupant—this was a new concept for me. All the women I knew were married, and those who lived by themselves were either widowed or elderly. Despite our age difference, Mrs. Ann took me under her wing, and I became her little protégé.

We did everything together. Mrs. Ann did not work outside the home, but she filled every day with shopping, visiting friends, or some fun activity. I observed how she moved, the words she used, and how she phrased her comments just so. There were confidence and grace in everything she did. I witnessed another aspect of what it meant to be a woman.

Every other week she had an appointment to get her hair done, and since I was her mentee, I also had an appointment. Tall of stature, hair perfectly coiffured, and café-au-lait skin,

I thought she was so beautiful. Possessing a personal sense of style, she knew how to accessorize an outfit to make a fashion statement.

One day, while preparing for an outing, I chose a pair of casual slacks and a chocolate brown top to complete my outfit. For me, clothing was purely functional: Quality was the primary prerequisite, followed by "Is it practical?"

After dressing, I went downstairs, and Mrs. Ann gave me a look that said something was amiss. What was it? I did not know, but I was soon to receive my first lesson in style. She said, "Carolyn, that brown top is too close to your natural skin tone." How was I to know this was a problem? And besides, "What does that mean, anyway?"

I was hearing a concept for the first time. I purchased all my clothing at the Company Store, the backbone of every coal mining community. There we made a selection from the limited number of items on display. The Company Store, owned and operated by the coal mine, was the heart of commercial activity for the miners and their families. It was the supermarket, the department store, the hardware store, and in many cases, the banking institution.

This hub of society was where I purchased the "what not to wear" dark chocolate brown top. Mr. Burbish and Mr. Mattney, two men over sixty, made the selection. Neither of them was fashion-savvy like Mrs. Ann. It went into the trash, as it did not meet Mrs. Ann's approval! It would be years before I wore any garment of a brown hue.

COLOR MAKES A DIFFERENCE

My takeaway from my first lesson in becoming fashionable: The palette of my wardrobe makes a difference. Color can enhance or take away from my natural beauty. Mrs. Ann schooled me on shades of color and how to select tones that could transform me from drab to stylish. This introductory lesson in color analysis taught me the colors which flatter my natural skin tone.

Mrs. Ann became my fashion mentor, and I became an eager student; she changed the way I viewed clothing. Over the next couple of weeks, she used pictures in fashion magazines to explain why an outfit was stylish. Also, I learned the value of purchasing clothing in *my* colors. Building a wardrobe around my specific color scheme guarantees that most items are interchangeable, which means more versatility in my outfits.

Another important principle for building a stunning wardrobe: only purchase clothing that looks good on you, not the current fashion. It is better to maintain my personal style than to follow the latest fad. Following this tip, I presently have items in my wardrobe that are over thirty years old.

One more style tip—we should only buy what we love! If we love it, our confidence goes up a couple of notches. According to Mrs. Ann, any woman can be stylish and fashionable; simply dress for her body type and colors. The goal of fashion is to assemble an outfit that says, *wow*! And style is a learned skill that anyone can learn, even if I am from West Virginia. What a powerful lesson.

LEARNING CAN HAPPEN AT ANY MOMENT

On an ordinary morning, my mindset shifted from being fashionably ordinary to fashionably elegant. The actress Audrey Hepburn, playing Holly Golightly's role in *Breakfast at Tiffany's,* eventually became my fashion inspiration. The character's classic and effortless style moved me to purchase pearls in every color and length possible. I love pearls because of Holly Golightly!

My trip to Connecticut was a turning point for me in many ways. Yes, I had the opportunity to have a real vacation and meet new people—but more importantly, I had inadvertently enrolled in a personal development program. I learned how to make a great first impression and become a stylish, confident young lady.

My fashion journey was only beginning. When I returned home, my mother had some changes in store for me as well. It was time to move beyond the company Store's fashion selections with Mr. Burbish and Mr. Mattney as fashion consultants.

Now, I purchased my clothing at the Smartwear Shop. This was a stylish lady's boutique in downtown Mullens. They carried the best brands and the latest fashions. It was where the movers and shakers in the city purchased their daughters' clothing.

Why the change? That fall, I attended Ben Dunman Junior High School in downtown Mullens. This school was in a new city with a new set of friends; in other words, much of my life was about to change.

Mullens was a thriving little city with brick homes, street lamps, traffic lights, and an actual bank. All the commercial conveniences we would expect were located there: a G.C. Murphy's Five and Dime, a Piggly Wiggly grocery store, jewelry and hardware stores, and specialty dress shops for men and women.

This city was a drastic change from my rural community, where streets were unnamed and pitch-black at night. When compared to my small town, I attended school in a major metropolis. My future classmates were the sons and daughters of businessmen, teachers, and other professionals. But there were also children like me, the daughter of a coal miner and a day worker. For these reasons, my mother thought a new wardrobe was in order.

The summer of 1963 filled my young life with change and several first-time experiences. And we tend to remember any first-time event. Most memorable that summer were the two women who shaped my sense of fashion and style. My makeover began with Mrs. Ann. She took a little country girl, validated her uniqueness, and taught her to make a chic first impression and be visible in a crowd. My confidence rose to a new level. As a mentor, she simply shared information she used every day. Her expertise empowered me to blossom into a confident young lady.

Next, my mother knew that clothes could enhance my self-esteem and confidence. When we look our best, we tend to perform our best. Edith Head, the American costume designer, is quoted as saying, "You can have anything you want in life if you dress for it." I don't know if I fully agree with that statement, but her point is this: Clothing can boost any woman's confidence. And there are times when that is precisely what we need.

Today, many young girls never experience an initial fashion lesson, as Mrs. Ann shared with me. They miss the opportunity to develop their distinctive style. That lesson is a confidence-builder, which is essential to their growth and development.

When we understand that every young lady is an original, we automatically reject the idea of being a carbon copy of someone else. Fashion then takes on new meaning and becomes an expression and a celebration of our uniqueness. My mother also taught me a valuable lesson: Sometimes, we need to dress for success to be successful.

> *"Always be the first-rate version of yourself and
> not the second-rate version of someone else."*
>
> —Judy Garland

TABLE TALK:

How would you describe your sense of style, and what is your favorite accessory?

5

WHAT GOOD ARE MANNERS?

Good manners prepare us to walk through an open door.

In 1966, America was experiencing a tumultuous social, political, and economic shift. Lyndon B. Johnson was president, civil rights protests were occurring in the South, astronauts conquered outer space, a war brewed in Vietnam, and the prominent public figure Malcolm X was assassinated.

America was in a crisis, and drastic changes can make or break a country and its people. These events made up the historical backdrop as I learned to be an adult. That year I turned fourteen and experienced some life changes of my own.

For me, coming of age signaled independence and permission to take some actions for the first time. Two seemingly insignificant yet influential incidents for a young girl come to mind. First was permission to wear high heels. Heels signified adulthood, and in my household, fourteen was the magic number for this to occur.

Second, I could pierce my ears. Having pierced ears was fashionable at the time, and I could not wait. I was permitted to wear small gold hoops, but earrings that dangled from my ear lobe were forbidden. Those were reserved for mature women. Since I was only fourteen, it didn't include me.

The origin of these guidelines was unknown to me, but all the women I knew accepted and followed them. According to an "unwritten rule book," an entirely white ensemble is the appropriate church attire on Easter Sunday. Then the rules change. An all-white outfit is unacceptable until Memorial Day. Between Memorial Day and Labor Day, white is chic and fashionable. But after Labor Day, it was a no-no. Rules, rules, and more rules. What's more, a lady wore nylon stockings, even when the thermometer reached ninety degrees in August.

COMING OF AGE

For me, wearing high heels and having pierced ears were rites of passage. They marked an unspoken agreement that I was approaching adulthood and ready to manage the changing world around me.

Yes, I was a year older, but what else was required to close the gap between childhood and adulthood? To be honest, I wasn't sure I was ready. I asked the same questions that every teenager ponders.

Who was I becoming?
Where was I going?
What values and actions would take me there?

In other words—I was being stretched to grow. That year I would enter my final year of junior high. Soon I would be in high school, thinking about graduation, considering colleges and what career path I would pursue. I was becoming a young adult who needed to plan. What would help me thrive during this transition?

My social circle soon extended beyond the nurturing close-knit community in which I grew up. It was time to step outside my comfort zone with confidence. For an introvert, this coming-of-age process was awkward since social settings were often uncomfortable for me. I needed a strategy that would allow me to embrace new people and situations with ease, handle my social fears, and learn others' expectations.

I chose an unlikely crutch: etiquette. This choice would serve me in three ways. First, it allowed me to move beyond my place of comfort and ensure I wouldn't become stuck. Second, it changed my focus from *me* to how I could influence others. And third, I gained self-assurance. When I felt I performed what others expected of me, I tended to relax. This plan provided the structure, rules, and guidelines I needed to face whatever life threw at me.

The website SocialMettle.com says, "Good manners define you as a person, while etiquette is what makes you socially acceptable."[5] Being courteous was expected behavior in our home. Greeting family members with a "good morning," saying "please," or "thank you," or holding a door for the person behind us was what we did. My mother insisted that her children were well-mannered, and we did not disappoint her. To her, rude behavior was unacceptable and an indication of a lack of parental oversight.

Being knowledgeable about manners was essential, but it did not prepare me for every social situation. I needed to go beyond "yes, ma'am" or "no, sir" and acquire the skill to interact and communicate on a deeper level. Etiquette is a code of conduct that empowers us to leverage relationships and influence outcomes.

The New Lexicon Webster's Dictionary of the English Language defines etiquette as 1) the rules of behavior standard in polite society and 2) the rules governing professional conduct.[6] Our English word is derived from a French word, which means ticket.

It is conduct or procedure associated with good breeding or prescribed as appropriate in social or official life. *The Random House Book of Etiquette* defines etiquette in three parts: manners, form, and usage.[7] The focal point is how we relate to others.

Form encompasses the established traditions of our society. And thirdly, usage entails knowledge of what is considered acceptable today. My definition is "the ability to enhance interaction with another individual and extract the benefits that connection offers." It is the mutual collaboration between two individuals.

Rules are constantly changing. Every generation decides how formal or informally they choose to live—but the main objective is for two individuals to find agreement instead of focusing on their differences.

MY JOURNEY BEGINS

During my fourteenth year, I built upon my mother's instruction and increased my knowledge surrounding etiquette. I prefer to say that I learned how to become a skilled collaborator. This capacity was a positive response to my fear of uncomfortable social situations. Simply put, I knew what was socially or professionally acceptable and then did it, intending to eliminate any potential disagreement and find common ground. Etiquette allows two parties to maintain their core values and develop beneficial partnerships.

I found answers to my questions in books from the school library, in Miss Manners articles, and of course, by asking my mother. Since she catered food events for the business community, she knew what they expected.

For instance, I learned which fork to use with a salad or main course and how to set the dinner table, placing glasses in their proper positions. Other rules included the appropriate sequence for introductions and making small talk (which I am still mastering). I used these tools when the situation required them to break down barriers.

Understanding the importance of etiquette became more significant in high school. I was involved in Thespians, the French club, marching band, and flag team. These extracurricular activities offered opportunities to travel and meet new people. Each experience brought adventure, excitement, and learning, but I had an awareness that socially I had some growing to do.

Of course, these emotions are typical for most teenagers, but I felt them intensely because I was the only student, or one of only a few, African Americans in these groups. Being an introvert in a world that prefers charismatic extroverts, I struggled.

ANY SKILL CAN SERVE AS A TOOL

How do we manage uncomfortable feelings when in surroundings that are foreign to us? How does an introvert compensate for the loud conversations that have no substance? Etiquette helped me bridge the gap. It served as a guide when I wondered what actions to take in unfamiliar situations.

A year later, I had the opportunity to test my social skills on a new level when an organization called Up with People came to our community. I do not recall the details of the group, but they offered personal development and leadership training. One such opportunity was a leadership gathering in Charleston, West Virginia.

The venue was a mansion with manicured lawns, an in-ground swimming pool, and hors d'oeuvres served by white-coated waiters to people whose attire said *wealthy*. Jay Rockefeller, who later served as senator and governor of West Virginia, was present and even shook my hand.

Remember, I grew up in a coal camp! Meeting a future governor, let alone someone named Rockefeller was not on my radar. It was my social skills rooted in good manners and etiquette that kept my feet on the ground. I appeared confident and unshaken, but inside, I thought, *how did I get here?*

Later that year, I took my first airplane ride. I was lucky to have the window seat, which gave me a view of the world at thirty-five thousand feet. The world looks different from that altitude. What a view! My destination was an *Up with People* event on Mackinac Island in Michigan, a beautiful seaside resort on Lake Huron. The entire trip was a memorable event for me.

That summer, I worked as a volunteer on program activities, attended leadership workshops, stayed in the historic Grand Hotel, and met individuals from all over the country. The evenings were filled with fun, musicals, and plays, all at no charge. Harry Belafonte's wife (at that time) was a guest during my stay, and one evening I was seated for dinner at her table.

I now possessed the self-confidence to connect with people and make friends in an unfamiliar environment. Knowing which fork to use, what to do with my napkin, and how to make small talk allowed me to relax and take advantage of this opportunity. More importantly, I learned to push past my fears and rise up with courage. Change requires self-discipline and taking responsibility for our perceived limitations and self-doubt.

My mother's instruction prepared me for a life she would never experience. Why insist on teaching me social skills? Did I need them in Alpoca, West Virginia? Not at all! But she saw a glimpse of my future. It demanded that I change my frame of reference and seek to influence my environment positively.

Supreme Court Justice Clarence Thomas said, "Good manners will open doors that the best education cannot."[8] This statement is so true. If we refer to the earlier definition of etiquette from the root word meaning ticket, it empowers us to function.

A ticket gives us access. Once we enter, we have permission to participate and experience life on a deeper level. The venue may be entertainment, education, politics, or a social event—it does not matter. Any acquired skill can offer us admission.

Furthermore, once we have entrée, there are resources and relationships at our disposal. These are the tools that can catapult us to success. The talent and acquired skills we possess are tools; they open up possibilities to achieve our goals. Sometimes, in life, we need a ticket to access available resources.

> A TICKET ALLOWS ONE ACCESS TO A VENUE AND ALL THE BENEFITS AVAILABLE WITHIN THAT VENUE.

What ability, talent, or skill can you use to find commonality with others? Use it to open doors.

"When I dare to be powerful, to use my strength in the service of my vision, then it becomes less and less important whether I am afraid."

—Audre Lord

TABLE TALK:

What strategies have you used to diminish social awkwardness in unfamiliar situations?

PART TWO
CHOOSING OUR VALUES

Our values serve as an internal operating system that monitors our thought processes and responses to life situations—similar to a computer's operating system. Its programming controls the computer's function, and it will only complete the tasks installed.

Our value system similarly serves us—as a guide and reminder for the predetermined vision of our expectations and the boundaries significant to us. These values become our prearranged or automatic responses. Values and boundaries allow us to live authentic lives where our behavior aligns with *who we say we are.*

With a system properly installed and functioning, we can model our best selves and influence others. Our values are the road map to success and serve as reminders that we were created to make a difference.

1

GIVING WHAT WE WANT TO RECEIVE

Self-awareness is a check-up from the neck up.

Who are we becoming? *Becoming* a person of destiny hinges on the daily decisions we make. Are we intentionally choosing to reach our potential? Are we living at our best, or are we distracted by an event that disrupts our daily process?

The goal of self-awareness is to provide an opportunity to conduct a mental or emotional check-up. Am I successfully managing distractions and my emotions? Am I intentionally choosing to live within my values, or am I making excuses for my behavior? The results of this check-up will reveal where we are in the process, plus the adjustments needed.

In my junior year of high school, I had the opportunity to learn this valuable lesson. I remember arguing with a classmate in the girls' bathroom. Nothing life-shattering; in fact, I don't recall precisely what the spat was about.

We exchanged words with raised voices, and in the heat of the moment, our anger became a distraction from the potential we both possessed. Anger is an emotion that sends us onto a sharp detour. I didn't see it coming, but suddenly it was there, demanding my attention. I was offended by her comments, and she was offended by mine, yet neither of us would back down.

As our emotions escalated, a teacher came in. With a stern look, her expression was a reminder to compose ourselves and move on. Leaving that room, I was determined to win at any cost. What strategy would give me the upper hand? My solution—I would ignore my antagonist, giving her the cold shoulder. I would refuse to speak to her! That would even the score, in my mind, and win the battle. This was the logic of an immature teenager whose feelings were hurt!

LIFE IS ABOUT THE CHOICES WE MAKE

How my attitude affected my enemy, I do not know. But, it was affecting me. Something was not right; an internal conflict raged inside me and tested my character. I was winning the battle, yet losing the war—I would be the only true casualty.

Questions began to swirl in my mind. *Who was I? How far was I willing to go to win a battle? Did I like the person I was becoming?* I had to decide. Did I have the strength to change course and adhere to the principles essential to the person I wanted to become? The other option was to emulate my offender and perpetrate unkindness with a poor attitude, making others miserable.

For weeks I chose to be unkind to another human being and justified my actions. My behavior was an indicator of where I needed to adjust and make strategic corrections to get back on track. This process revealed that negative energy is unproductive and emotionally draining. What a rude awakening. I remember the ladies at the table saying that "ugly is as ugly does."

Thankfully, my mother was unaware of my actions. She would disapprove and categorize it as unbecoming. Life reveals who we are, and when we are becoming something other than who we planned, it is time to change.

YOU HAVE THE POWER TO CHOOSE

Decisions, decisions, decisions. I decided to take control and move in the opposite direction—*give out what I want to receive*. As stated in Galatians 6:7b, "A man reaps what he sows" (NIV). I took a one-hundred-eighty degree turn and changed my perspective.

This lifestyle reversal was not conditional or based on the merit of the individual. No, I chose to live by my beliefs, lay down the hatchet, and forgive my offender. I would be kind, friendly, and forgiving because that is who I am.

The other girl responded with kindness to that attitude adjustment. We never became best friends, but I learned a valuable lesson—I **can** choose to treat others with respect and compassion.

Life is about making hard decisions, and the right ones are not always easy, nor are they always reciprocated. However, this was more about *me becoming me*. Fulfilling my purpose and my values outweighed any reward I could have received. If authenticity and growth are the end goals, we must do what is suitable for us, regardless of the other person's behavior or outcome.

WE HAVE THE POWER TO MAKE THE RIGHT CHOICE

This philosophy allows me to update my operating system and model my best behavior continuously. For me, life is the sum of my decisions and the choices I made. Hopefully, others will recognize that they have options in life as well.

Dr. Frank Crane, a Presbyterian minister and columnist states, "The Golden Rule is of no use to us whatsoever unless we realize that it's our move!"[9] We all have the power to make the first move. I decided to move *first* only because I heard my mother's wise counsel whispering in my ear. Those words continue to shape my decisions. And sometimes, we need a gentle reminder to stay on track.

"Don't compromise yourself—you're all you have."

—John Grisham

TABLE TALK:

Describe an incident that tested your values. What did you learn from this experience?

2

GOSSIP HURTS

Gossip is the inability to control our mind and our tongue.

Today, most of the world communicates through cell phones. We are connected, even when we prefer not to be. Alexander Graham Bell started a revolution when he called his assistant, Mr. Watson, on a telephone he named a "sound telegraph" in 1876. Since then, the communication industry has evolved many times.

I remember the black rotary dial phone sitting on an end table in my parents' living room and having a party line. A party line was a phone line shared by multiple users. These were popular as I grew up. It allowed the telephone company to serve rural communities at a reduced cost to the consumer and the company.

One of the significant inconveniences or drawbacks to the party line was the lack of privacy. Anyone on our line could pick up their phone and listen to our conversation. Consequently, party lines contributed to the spread of gossip. To eavesdrop on a conversation without being exposed required skill.

The individual wanting to listen in had to pick up their receiver gently, so there was no corresponding *click*. Then, they could listen undetected. The only give-away was background noise on their end. In our small community, the party line was a source of idle talk circulating; gossip started with one person eavesdropping on a conversation not intended for them.

GOSSIP IS IDLE TALK

Gossip is idle talk, or unproductive conversation focused on the personal or private affairs of others. It may involve exaggeration, half-truths, manipulation of facts, or an outright lie. The words are secondary; the fundamental principle is how it affects the lives of individuals. Gossip is dangerous because it can harm people. Each retelling chips away at a person's potential and destroys their self-esteem. Idle words are powerful.

A rumor may start to undermine an enemy or someone who is the object of jealousy. The ladies at the table considered it unattractive to participate in such activities. If I heard it once, I heard it a thousand times: *"If you can't say something good about someone, don't say anything at all."*

Every person must take responsibility for their words because misdirected conversations are harmful. It requires discipline to avoid gossip because it's easy to offer our opinion in the exchange. Once gossip starts, it gathers momentum, moving with greater intensity, and becomes impossible to stop. The easiest way to avoid this trap is to stop before it begins.

Sometimes, it is difficult to withhold our opinion or what initially sounds like a simple comment or observation. But our response reveals our lack of integrity. Will we engage in gossip or withdraw from the unhealthy conversation? If we consider the other person and figuratively stand in their shoes, we can refuse to join the discussion.

The ladies at our table were wise women and lived what they preached. They were cautious around those who kept the grapevine humming. They believed those who engaged talebearers would soon become the object of their wagging tongues. Anyone who gossips *with* me will gossip *about* me. Their advice, "avoid them like the plague."

Mrs. Sara, we will call her, was one such neighbor. People knew her as a gossip carrier. I don't recall ever seeing her seated at my mother's kitchen table. My mother was kind and helpful to her family, yet there was always an unspoken lack of trust between Mrs. Sara and the ladies. Even as a child, I knew to be polite yet maintain my distance.

SPEAK WORDS OF ENCOURAGEMENT

Our words can build up or tear down. They have a positive or negative impact on those who hear them. Talk can equip, encourage, celebrate, or inspire others. Only we can decide how we'll use our words. Are our conversations instruments of positive change? Or, will we, seeking to bolster our self-confidence, use them to destroy someone else? This lesson is hard to learn because negative conversations subtly pull us in.

Remember, gossip's ultimate aim is to destroy a person's self-esteem and ability to be productive. To avoid this, simply recall the advice of the ladies at the table: *"If you can't say something good, don't say anything at all."*

> *"Great minds discuss ideas; average minds discuss events; small minds discuss people."*
>
> —Eleanor Roosevelt

TABLE TALK:

Share a time when you were on the receiving end of gossip. How did it make you feel? How did you respond?

3

TELLING TIME TO BE ON TIME

I'm late; I'm late for a very important date.

—The White Rabbit in *Alice in Wonderland.*

Late is a missed opportunity to shine.

P unctuality is one of my strengths. It is a trait I learned from my father, who, to my knowledge, was never late. If we were attending an event, we were always on time and usually the first to arrive. Being fashionably late was never an option. Either we were on time, or we did not attend.

For me, arriving fifteen minutes early is a must. Those extra minutes allow for unexpected traffic delays, finding the correct address, securing a parking space, locating the meeting room, and a quick visit to the ladies' room to freshen my makeup.

Those extra minutes are unnecessary for some, but for me, they are the very difference between success and failure. They alleviate the hustle and bustle of rushing at the last minute. I am just like my father—I hate being late!

SOME SUBJECTS ARE DIFFICULT

It is challenging to be on time if we cannot look at our watch to determine the time of day. We use the concept of time to give our lives context—so we know when to interact with the world around us. This construct allows us to show up when someone expects us and leave in time to arrive at our next appointment.

Humanity has used various methods to tell time throughout history. Long ago, it was the moon and stars or the sun's position in the sky. Whatever way we choose, the goal is to get to our destination early or on time and not be late. The entire world runs on this system of noting the hours and minutes.

Telling time is a simple exercise that many children learn with ease. Not me. In the third grade, I struggled and could only make sense of the clock face if the hour and minute hands squarely pointed to a number. Even though I excelled in school, I was unable to comprehend the terms "quarter after," "half past," and "quarter till." Phrases like "twenty after" or "twenty till" were also complicated.

Confused and frustrated, I failed assignments. Nothing made sense. On numerous occasions, my parents and teacher explained the concepts, but I was unsuccessful in comprehending the idea each time. As other students grasped the lesson and were ready to move on, I became increasingly self-conscious.

Soon, I received a lesson on telling time that changed everything for me. It was not a tutoring session arranged by my parents or my teacher. Like so many others, it was an ordinary day, yet this one would have a different outcome.

I was sitting on the front porch with my mother when I saw Mrs. Janie walking toward our house. She was barefoot, as usual, with a couple of her children following her. Mrs. Janie was coal-black in color, with coal-black hair, white teeth, a sharp nose, and thin lips. Beautiful features or good bones, as they say in the modeling profession.

She was an attractive woman with the habit of going barefoot during the summer. She didn't even wear flip-flops. Everyone I knew wore shoes, except Mrs. Janie. To me, this was a peculiar habit for an adult.

That day, she stopped at the front gate of our property to talk to my mother. They chatted for a while, and suddenly I realized I was the topic of the conversation. Somehow their conversation segued into my inability to tell time. Mrs. Janie opened the gate and took a seat beside me on the porch steps as her children played in the front yard.

"Go get a pencil and paper," she said. Off I went. I did not ask questions; an adult had given me a command, and I obeyed. When I returned, the two of us sat on the front steps, and she proceeded to teach a lesson on how to tell time.

On the paper, Mrs. Janie drew the diagram of a clock, with the numbers one through twelve, and explained how to measure time on the clock face. The long hand indicates the minute hand, and the short hand indicates the hour.

The lesson continued as she explained that sixty minutes equal an hour and that it takes sixty minutes for the long hand to make a full rotation of the clock to move the short hand from one minute to the next.

Next, Mrs. Janie explained, whichever number the minute hand pointed to represented how many minutes had passed, which was always in multiples of five. She asked, "Do you know how to count by fives?" I did, of course, but she had me recite my five multiplication tables to make sure.

Mrs. Janie followed up with a lesson explaining the dreaded quarter past, half past, quarter till, and what they meant. As she talked, she drew diagrams to illustrate what each one meant. Slowly, these strange concepts began to make sense, and my feeling of confidence grew.

Mrs. Janie and I sat on the steps for what seemed like hours while she drew different clock faces, answered my questions, and gave me exercises to make sure I understood. When she ended our lesson and left, I confidently said, "I can tell time!"

Why was Mrs. Janie able to do, in a couple of hours, what my teacher and parents had not been able to do? I believe it was the individualized attention—her ability to identify and address what I did not understand, that moved the needle for me. I worked at my own pace, thought through the concepts, and visualized connections in my mind. Her drawings and diagrams were a game-changer.

Knowing how we process information allows us to approach learning from a position of strength. That experience revealed that I am a visual learner—one whose comprehension is enhanced when visually engaged. This individualized learning strategy enabled me to comprehend what I previously couldn't grasp.

Mrs. Janie was not a trained educator, yet she employed a teaching principle that helped me switch from failing to thriving. In one day, my self-confidence shot through the roof. Nothing happens in life by chance. This meeting was no coincidence and changed my life. An ordinary woman had decided to elevate an everyday conversation and create my extraordinary outcome.

The time we spent on those steps allowed me to become an early arriver for any appointment. Every encounter has learning potential and can change lives if we listen for the needs and share our knowledge or solutions to help others succeed.

In life, our paths will cross those who need a skill or talent we possess. I am grateful Mrs. Janie invested in a little girl who desperately needed an impromptu tutor. Her instruction made all the difference to me. It would be impossible to arrive fifteen minutes early if I never learned to tell time!

"Early is on time, on time is late, and late is unacceptable."

—Eric Jerome Dickey

TABLE TALK:

Describe an incident that challenged you to learn a new skill.

4

LEARNING TO FORGIVE: SOMEONE WILL DISAPPOINT ME

Forgiveness is deciding to let go.

My mother is one of the most amazing women I know. She is strong, loving, resourceful, and opinionated. If there is a problem, she will find a solution and do it with a smile. Defeat is not in her vocabulary. So, I was alarmed one day when I came home and saw her crying. I had never seen my mother cry, and I didn't understand why she was now.

Mrs. White, a lady she worked for as a domestic, accused her of stealing and then fired her. As a child, my mother was the most beloved person in the world to me; so, when she cried, it shook me. I was emotionally devastated, and at that moment, our roles reversed. I became the protector, mentally preparing to confront her accuser. I have a dominant, take-charge personality, so coming to my mother's defense was an easy step for me.

A FALSE ACCUSATION

Anyone who knew my mother would realize this accusation was false. She was industrious, a person of character and integrity, and inclined to give rather than receive. A person's name and reputation were assets she guarded like money in the bank. She instructed her children on the virtues of honesty versus lying—the importance of being a giver and not stealing—which she never tolerated.

Once, she took one of my siblings who had stolen by the hand and marched them back to the store to confess taking candy without paying for it. That confession was followed by an apology to the proprietor and punishment when they returned home. I didn't forget that lesson.

Seeing my mother cry was troubling. It was disturbing because the accusation was unjustified. My anger exploded inside me, and I was determined to seek revenge. Mrs. White had incriminated my mother, brought shame to our family, and I wanted her to pay. She deserved it! However, my mother taught me another valuable lesson. Life is not fair, and sometimes, bad things happen to good, honest people.

REVENGE IS NEVER AN OPTION

Revenge was not my mother's objective. First, she knew her friends and the other families for whom she worked would never believe the lie, and they did not. A woman of integrity, Mother's life spoke volumes about who she was. Those who knew her rallied around her. In a small town, where everyone knows everyone and everything, their support was invaluable. Yet the emotional trauma of the allegation was borne by my mother, alone.

My mother believed Mrs. White would eventually find the item, so she continued to hold her head high, choosing not to carry a grudge against the accuser. When confronted with injustice, we can respond in the same spirit or decide to take the higher road—one that people don't often travel.

One day, my mother received a call from Mrs. White, reporting she had found the missing item. She apologized for her error and the embarrassment her actions caused. Then, she dared to ask my mother to resume working for her. My mother graciously accepted the apology but declined the offer of work and never mentioned the incident again. My mother's prayers were answered.

Years later, Mrs. White called my mother and asked if she would help her for one day. Of course, I thought, "The nerve of that woman!" That was not my mother's response. Mrs. White was elderly and declining in health, so my mother agreed to work for one day. She **chose** not to reciprocate. Her behavior is a clue to who she is. All my life, I observed her helping others, whether they deserved it or not. She was a caring person before, during, and after that accusation. She is who she is.

LEARN TO FORGIVE

I learned a valuable lesson.

My mother forgave, refused to hold a grudge, and helped the accuser who needed help. When I asked her about her response, she stated that in life, people will disappoint us. People make mistakes, but it is up to us to do unto others as we want them to do unto us. This biblical principle sounds simple, but of course, it is easier said than done. Besides, Mother didn't convince me that it was an appropriate response to a false accusation.

> FORGIVENESS IS ALWAYS APPROPRIATE.

Since that time, I have learned the principle she wanted me to grasp. I can **choose** to forgive, or I can seek revenge. I decide. I can walk in forgiveness and love or carry the ball and chain inscribed with *revenge, hate, rejection*, or any other negative emotion I want around me, dragging me down.

President Nelson Mandela modeled this principle on a national scale in South Africa. I have visited South Africa many times and am awed by the people's love and respect for him. This melting pot of indigenous Blacks, Coloreds, Indians, and Afrikaners refers to him as the Father of the Nation.

The political system of apartheid marred the nation's history until President Mandela united his country through forgiveness. He forgave his captors, even after twenty-six years of wrongful imprisonment.

Most individuals would find it difficult to absolve their enemies, yet Mandela said, "It always seems impossible until it's done."[10] Nothing is impossible! We can respond to injustice with actions that advance peace and reconciliation—even when forgiveness is underserved.

Negative emotions are destiny killers that divert our attention from creating positive change. Mrs. White could not distract my mother or send her on an unproductive detour. Love, compassion, and forgiveness are gifts she offers at will— what a powerful life lesson. We can provide a remarkable offering—forgiveness.

We choose how and when to model the beliefs that are important to us. If we value kindness, that becomes our gift. In a conflict, we can take the road that few of us travel, and our actions will speak volumes about who we are. The choice is always ours.

Life experiences can only hold us captive if we decide to remain a prisoner. Maya Angelou said, "Do the best you can until you know better. Then when you know better, you do better."[11] The question we must ask is, "Am I willing to forgive because I know better?" We never know until someone tests us. I can honestly say I saw this principle modeled by someone who wanted to teach *me* a valuable lesson.

"Forgiveness is not an occasional act; it is a constant attitude."

—Dr. Martin Luther King

TABLE TALK:

Describe a time someone falsely accused you. How did it make you feel?

5

MAKING THE RIGHT CHOICE

Choice is the ability to weigh our options and select the
outcome before we begin.

Wouldn't it be great to live impulsively, without a care about tomorrow? Isn't fun, personal happiness, and freedom the goal in life? Why can't we do whatever we want? Having dessert for breakfast sounds like a great idea. Ask any kid, and they would agree! Many individuals live their lives from that perspective. Their goal is to follow the idiom "Let's eat, drink, and be merry."

However, all decisions create outcomes, which may yield desirable results, or devastating consequences. Newton's third law states that for every action, there is an equal and opposite reaction.[12] With maturity, we learn to weigh outcomes, intentionally craft a preferred future, and minimize risk. Therefore, it is necessary to develop critical thinking abilities and become proficient in determining the best choices for positive outcomes.

Every day, we make decisions, and hopefully, become skilled practitioners in the process. We make thousands of decisions during a twenty-four-hour period. Some are simple or insignificant (*will I eat dessert for breakfast?*). Others are weighty, with devastating consequences or risks. In one example, the financial investors from Bernie Madoff's Ponzi scheme may never recover their losses. Did they foresee this outcome and weigh all the options, or did they assume the risk was insignificant?

OUR CHOICES DEFINE US

Every decision either advances or delays the achievement of our goals. That is a bitter pill to swallow. Even unexpected or unsolicited life experiences can lead to negative consequences and require a response. Will this life-altering event birth a victim mentality, or will it catapult me toward greatness? It might not be fair, but we can choose how we respond.

The Hutu and Tutsi tribes chose forgiveness to absolve acts of violence suffered during the 1994 Rwandan genocide. That decision allowed tribe members to mend their differences and heal their nation. As noted earlier, Nelson Mandela forgave his captors, partnering with them to create a more equal and ethical government.

Nick Vujicic, born without limbs, chose to develop his communication skills, become an author, and travel the world as a motivational speaker. All of them could have asked, "Why me?" They would be justified in asking this question, but the more pertinent question could be, "What action or decision has the greatest potential for positive change?" Sometimes life happens, and we must decide how we respond.

The ladies at the table were quick to inform, "What you sow, you will also reap." In other words, every choice has a consequence or benefit. When we shift our focus to possibilities, we can anticipate what will generate our desired result. Understanding this concept requires an awareness of our current situation and what we expect to achieve. We can identify the needed strategies to achieve those results or what behaviors are unproductive and eliminate them. Self-leadership, the ability to manage one's self through excellent decisions, increases this probability of success.

CHOOSE WISELY

Wisdom hides within this simple statement I often heard *the ladies* say, "What you sow, you will also reap." They clearly recognized that every decision wavered between a benefit or an undesirable consequence. Whether we like it or not, we are stuck with the aftermath of our choices.

These women sometimes made poor choices. We all have. Some married too young, leaving dreams unfulfilled, or had less-than-perfect marriages. However, I remember their desire to mentor others, offer lessons in the decision-making process so others would benefit, and receive favorable outcomes. With encouragement and support, they willingly helped others move past the repercussions of a poor decision. Gathering the person in need, they built a wall of support, allowing them to regain their footing.

If someone needed motherly advice, that was given as well. Sometimes, it was a shoulder to cry on, a cooked meal, a cleaned house, a "little piece of change," or respite for a new mother, overcome with responsibility. Without support, some of our life choices result in devastation.

The ladies at our table provided a safe harbor to recover from mistakes, build resilience, and regain forward motion, never allowing adverse circumstances to define anyone. For those they mentored, they were women who gave, without passing judgment. They warned of consequences yet supported all through missteps, with encouragement to stand tall and keep trying!

These women made time and created a healing refuge for others. They provided a place to learn, evaluate situations, contemplate new options, and apply wisdom in finding the right choice.

> *"While we are free to choose our actions, we are not free to choose the consequences of our actions."*

> —Steven R. Covey

Table Talk:

In life, we make decisions every day, some greater than others. What major decision did you make that had a life-changing outcome?

6

LEAVING BREADCRUMBS TO MARK THE PATH

Legacy is the culmination of the life we lived.

L ying in bed on a cold winter morning, I heard my mother dressing. She put on her winter coat and hat, went down the street, and returned with two little boys. Billy Joe and Charlie Lee's father had left them sleeping while he headed off for his shift at the coal mines. According to the rumor mill, his wife had abandoned the family and lived in a city up north. The thought of a mother leaving her children was difficult to comprehend. To my seven-year-old mind, living without my mother was unimaginable and devastating.

The boys' father knew my mother would wake the boys, dress them, and bring them to her home soon after he went to work. She bathed, fed, and prepared them for school alongside her own children.

LEAVING MY IMPRINT ON THE WORLD

West Virginia winters are long and cold with buckets of snowfall. Trudging through the slush with two sleepy boys was a chore many would decline. What made my mom respond when she had four children of her own? These two little boys who belonged to someone else needed her. Therefore, Monday through Friday, her act of kindness provided stability in their lives.

Caring for Billy Joe and Charlie Lee was not an isolated incident. They were only one example of the children my mother, Mrs. Millie, helped and nurtured. She was born to be everyone's mother. Not every woman wears that title as well as my mom, but she did, proudly.

With an unlimited capacity for love and nurturing children, fatigue never had a chance. Nor did she neglect her children when others joined their breakfast table or shared Mrs. Millie's attention. There was always more than enough love and food to pass around.

As a parental figure, her mission was to equip children with practical life skills, preparing them to live their American dream. She modeled these principles and taught them with a firm yet loving hand. She found the right balance—never too much, and always the perfect blend of both.

Even when a child needed correction, she tempered it with love and clarity about what needed to change. Her favorite saying was, "You can never love a child too much." She believed patience and endless doses of love could change any life.

My mother celebrated her one-hundredth birthday on September 29th, 2020. Her zest for life is contagious. Much wisdom can be gained during one hundred years. The progress she has witnessed in her lifetime is astounding: men on the moon, the internet, virtual currency, and most of all, the first African American president. The world has transformed, but change initiates growth, and each transition gleans more wisdom to share with others.

MODELING MY LIFE MESSAGE

I can sum up my mother's message as, "Take personal responsibility for the community you belong to." We can empower people if we invest in their lives. The late Elijah Cummings, United States House of Representatives member from Maryland, once said, "Our children are the living messengers to the future that we will never see."

Mrs. Millie, my mother, is not a household name like Mr. Cummings, but they share a similar vision and passion to prepare and equip children for generations to come. The next generation serves as ambassadors, representing us—our values, beliefs, ethics, morals, and guiding principles—which creates continuity from this generation to the next.

My mother took personal responsibility for children in our community and invested in them. She created memories, love, protection, and connection with them. Many responded with a simple "thank you" or expressed gratitude for being one of *her* kids. One life *can* make a difference.

We must be passionate about helping those in need and committed to taking action that will change lives. To make a difference, leave an indelible impression on someone!

"We can make a difference, wherever we are," should be everyone's life message. It is easy to focus on what we don't have, but we each have talent and ability, a gift that permits us to empower the world. Our sphere of influence may differ from others, but what we offer and who we affect is a worthier pursuit.

One person can affect a few, while another can empower the world, yet each person must commit to change at least one person. If we help one person through acts of kindness, we contribute to bettering our world. We must embrace how we can contribute, stop comparing ourselves to others, and simply live our best life. Being the best we can be should be our ultimate goal.

Mission Impossible was a popular television show I enjoyed as a teenager. The program followed government agents on secret assignments, and each episode began with the same opening sequence. The team would receive their newest commission from a tape recording that would self-destruct after being played.

Each mission followed along the same theme: capture a spy, or help a dignitary in distress. The team could accept or refuse the assignment. However, if they refused, the consequence was disastrous for the government or a prominent official. But, if they accepted, they were guaranteed to rescue one person, and often they saved millions.

Our lives are similar, whether part of the *Mission Impossible* team or not. God created us to change lives and make the world a better place. We have a mission to accomplish but can refuse to accept it. The result of that decision might not defeat terrorists or prevent a government's collapse, but someone is waiting for our gift.

Our contributions won't appear on television or in movies, but they are equally impressive. If we refuse this assignment to live our best lives, we dimmish our legacy, and the world suffers without our unique contribution. We must show up, intentional and determined every day, to share our individual abilities. This is what legacy is all about.

"A life well-lived is the most exquisite work of art."

—Erwin McManus

TABLE TALK:

Everyone makes a first impression. In one sentence, write what you would like people to say about you.

PART THREE
BELIEVING IT'S POSSIBLE

Possibility is determined by our self-concept and how our previous and present experiences have influenced us. We are shaped by our environment, relationships, and innate personality. All these attributes contribute to the unique person identified as *me*. To maximize our potential for growth, it is important to evaluate who we are presently and where we desire to go.

Are we equipped with the personal qualities that empower us to succeed? Are we willing to ask ourselves challenging questions? *"Do my former beliefs, mindsets, and behaviors support me today? Will they permit me to reach my goals?"* Those answers will determine if we are prepared to change our frame of reference.

It's unproductive to dwell on our past failures and mishaps. That process only serves us when the objective is to learn from our mistakes and change our behavior where necessary. But it takes courage to step into the unfamiliar and believe what appears to be impossible is possible. What we can achieve *now* should be our objective.

My specialty will be different from someone else's because my abilities are unique, but the seeds of greatness are within. These areas of expertise grant us influence. We must believe that! The fundamental principles that require implementation to succeed are the mindset and attitude of a winner.

Focus on what is possible and move toward your goals. What you believe will motivate you to action. Are you committed to developing the skills required to succeed? Will you overcome adversity, hold yourself accountable to a mentor, learn from your mistakes, and keep moving forward? If so, then anything is possible!

1

TOMORROW WILL BE BETTER

Hope is knowing the best is yet to come.

I am waiting. For what? For things to change. The quiet of the four walls of my bedroom envelope me—the sounds of voices whose words are difficult to discern drift back to my room. Lying on my bed, I can hear the conversations of family members throughout the house. The hum of the refrigerator, the footsteps of people walking from one room to another, and the creaks and sounds an old house makes. I long to join my family, but I can't; I am recovering from surgery to remove a pilonidal cyst, and I am in pain.

Recovery is a slow process, and I ask myself, "When will this be over?" Frustration, despair, and even depression settle in because I am sick of being sick! When can I return to college? At that moment, feeling lost in my situation overwhelms me. As I listen to the flurry of activity in the house, my only option is to wait for my body to heal.

In my freshmen year of college, I dropped out to address this recurring health issue. As a youngster, I experienced typical childhood diseases: measles, mumps, and chickenpox passed from one household to the next. We simply waited our turn. Eventually, we caught whatever was going around because our friends had it. These temporary disruptors of childhood had one thing in common; they had a start and end date. Usually, fourteen days after our first symptom, we returned to regular activity. This short interlude was tolerable since we knew it would soon end.

That is excellent news because the country is a fun place for a child to grow up, and I don't want to miss anything. We can play softball and hide-n-seek, go fishing, build a makeshift cabin on the creek bank, or hang out with friends. I can sum up life as fun and freedom. But we have to remember one rule; be home before dark.

I also suffered from migraines, tonsillitis, numerous sore throats, and several lanced pilonidal cysts during my childhood. These health challenges resulted in me spending many days in bed, waiting to recover from the latest malady, which was not too difficult for an introvert. I could read, dream, and think to my heart's content.

But discouragement eventually consumed me because even an introvert who enjoys solitude desires it on their own terms. When illness took my freedom away, and I realized I had lost control, it felt like a prison. Plus, being physically uncomfortable was not fun.

During this recovery, I have vivid memories of my mother coming in to check on me. She was a welcomed guest, an interruption to the quietness. Her smile lifted my spirits and reminded me that I was not forgotten. God broke the mold when He created her—strong, determined, with a solution for any problem; she was also my nurse.

And twice a day, her visits indicated a painful dressing change was on the schedule. She followed the doctor's orders and was aware that a full recovery required following his protocol in detail. On those occasions, upon entering my room, she would say, "Tomorrow will be better." She repeated that phrase over and over again. More than encouraging words, they represented a philosophy that guided her worldview. She lived expecting tomorrow to be better than today.

For the next three months, those words became my silent prayer. "Yes, tomorrow will be better." She spoke those words day after day, building my faith, changing my outlook on life, and helping me visualize my healthy body. Pilonidal cysts heal slowly, even when following the prescribed protocol.

Every day, twice a day, my mother packed the incision with saltwater-saturated gauze. That was the most unpleasant part of my day. Imagine how upsetting this was for her. She had to perform an excruciatingly painful procedure essential to her child's recovery.

To lift my spirits, she gave updates on my progress. Sometimes she reported, "Oh, it's not as deep," or "It's not as red today." Each announcement gave me hope and built my faith for a full recovery. Day after day, I needed to believe that I would heal. That day eventually arrived, and the doctor released me to regular activity. I could finally return to college.

WE ARE NOT VICTIMS

A physical illness can be described as a persistent condition that disrupts normal activity because of pain or discomfort. A chronic condition may, over time, affect our perception of our future success. Will we reach our potential, or are we destined to victimization by a disease? My mother never allowed me to view myself as a victim. I was not permitted to feel sorry for myself. Therefore, I never thought I was unhealthy. That fact never occurred to me.

Dwelling on my health challenges was simply not tolerated. My mother believed my attitude was vital to my recovery. Would I develop the mindset of a champion or become a victim? Life is challenging, but when we envision tomorrow as better than our present circumstance, it increases our ability to persevere through adversity. This perspective allows us to live with hope!

That year, I learned a great deal about myself as a person and about life. First, I can choose to be optimistic about life. I did not say it was easy. It's far from it but necessary. I discovered that I have options amid a challenge and that changes my outlook on life. We can compare our existence to playing a game of cards with this adage; "we play the cards we're dealt." Eric, my husband, loves to play the card game Bid Whist.

To play, four players form teams of two, and each team works together to win seven points and win the game. An amazing fact about the game is the best hand does not guarantee a win. The skill of the players determines the outcome. A player who has mastered the game can take cards that are not considered "winners" and win.

They have learned to play the hand they were dealt—a difficult but necessary life lesson. Success requires resilience, endurance, and a focused mindset; these qualities prepare us to bounce back from adversity.

Second, I learned that expecting a better outcome implies pursuing solutions. This activity is not only positive thinking but developing strategies to address the issue. What is necessary to attain peak performance during the crisis? The objective is to move beyond being stuck. What is the best possible outcome for the situation? Can I eliminate or resolve it? What resources do I need, or who can assist? Or the question we never want to ask—must I learn to live with it?

Whatever solution we choose, our focus shifts from our present position to the place we desire to go. Personally, this process resulted in various behavioral and dietary changes. It was necessary to develop a regime that addressed my health issues. I eradicated some problems while merely managing others.

One key was eliminating dairy products from my diet. I eliminated foods that no longer contributed to my health—no more grilled cheese sandwiches, cottage cheese with fruit, or Oreo ice cream in a sugar cone. But these changes reaped fantastic results for me. I was determined to find a solution that permitted me to live as healthy as possible.

CHOOSE TO LIVE WITH HOPE

Dr. Paul G. Stoltz, who originated the *Adversity Quotient*, believes adversity strengthens and improves our capacity to excel in life by pushing and compelling us to go further.[13] Ultimately, adversity moves us beyond what is naturally comfortable to a position suitable for growth.

A crisis can mold and shape us into better versions of ourselves. I wish there were a more comfortable framework to follow. But most successful individuals have overcome adversity in their lifetime.

My husband, Eric Warren, is an example of someone who has triumphed over adversity. He grew up in poverty and a broken home but chose not to become a victim. He graduated from college, became a business owner, and served as a pastor for a church. But he considers his most significant achievements to be remaining faithful as a husband for fifty-plus years, a devoted father, grandfather, and great-grandfather.

He allowed childhood trauma to launch his potential instead of paralyzing him. Life will ask each one of us to write the final chapter of our personal journey through adversity. Will we be the hero or the victim?

When adversity strikes, we need someone to support, challenge and encourage us. For me, that person is my mother. She challenges me to believe that tomorrow will be better.

"With everything that has happened to you, you can either feel sorry for yourself or treat what has happened as a gift. Everything is either an opportunity to grow or an obstacle to keep you from growing. You get to choose."

—Dr. Wayne W. Dyer

TABLE TALK:

Describe a crisis you experienced and the learning that resulted.

2

UNLOCKING OUR GIFT

Excellence is using all our skills to create a thing of beauty.

There is a remarkable quality that sets us apart. We are unique human beings, created to make contributions to the world with confidence. Our purpose is hidden in what we do well.

What do you do that, when finished, people respond, "Wow! That was great." At that moment, you made a difference, and you may have discovered your gift.

The women at the table were a diverse group who migrated to a community because their husbands worked at the local coal mine. They differed in height from short to tall; personalities included quiet and outgoing, and skin tones spanned every shade of brown from dark chocolate to light vanilla. They were physically different but also uniquely gifted.

Mrs. Eunice excelled at canning and preserving food. If we needed a jar of canned tomatoes or green beans, we knew where to go. Every year she and her husband demonstrated their green thumbs by growing a vegetable garden overflowing with produce.

Mrs. Ruth kept a watchful eye on everyone's children. One look or word from her was sufficient to prevent mischief and made every parent's job a little easier. Mrs. Helen, the

Sunday school teacher, was determined that each child have a Christian foundation.

She organized the Easter and Christmas plays, and every child had a part. This guaranteed Mt. Olivet Baptist Church was packed with members and nonmembers to see their children perform. Mrs. Janie was sharp-witted and prepared with comments that made us chuckle. But behind the jests were insights that invited consideration. She also had a gift for making sure no one took themselves too seriously.

DISCOVERING OUR GIFTS

My mother's gift was cooking, and she loved it. She jumped at the opportunity to prepare an entrée or dessert for a church event or someone in need. Often, a neighbor who was not feeling well would request that my mom send them a dinner. They knew we had plenty, and whatever was on the menu that day would be scrumptious. She would lovingly prepare a plate of delicious food and send one of my brothers to deliver it to their door.

Mother acquired the skill of cooking from her father, who was a chef. As a young lady, she worked in restaurants, honing her culinary knowledge. One piece of information that became her signature was the importance of plating food. The presentation of an entrée differentiates a casual or fine dining experience. Food must taste delicious, but the presentation elevates the meal and makes it a memorial event. The aroma and appearance create the initial invitation to take that first bite. If it does not look or smell appealing, no one desires to eat it.

Holiday meals were special events for my mother. She left nothing to chance. She began mulling over a holiday menu a month in advance. Once she chose an entrée, she selected vegetables to compliment the meat. She sought to create the perfect plate—an entrée accented by beautiful colors on a china canvas.

A plate lacking in color was a cardinal sin. The goal was to present a dish with superb ingredients and contrasting elements. The final product was a work of art with color, texture, and aroma. Her heart was in her work; the last step for the masterpiece was to wipe the rim clean.

DO EVERYTHING WITH JOY

When we express our gifts with joy, our contributions bring happiness to others. My mother knew where she excelled, and that gave her satisfaction. But more importantly, was the joy she experienced watching others consume her food. Eventually, she started a small catering business that served business leaders in our community. She loved every minute of it.

As a child, I helped my mother prepare hors d'oeuvres for catering events. I was not fond of this task. Making vegetable trays was not my idea of fun. There were times I had to recut carrots, celery sticks, or potatoes because they were not uniform in size.

She also loved working into the wee hours of the morning and seemed to become more energized as the night went on. I, on the other hand, wanted to go to bed at a decent hour. My mother demanded excellence, and what was she expecting from the diner who consumed a meal? A question that she loved to hear, "May I have seconds, please?"

DO EVERYTHING WITH A SPIRIT OF EXCELLENCE

Life lessons can be acquired in the most unlikely circumstances. Even when we do not enjoy the task we are doing. Observing my mother, I learned it is essential to know what I do well and then *do it well!* Whatever I commit to should produce something of outstanding quality—nothing less.

Mediocrity is never an option because our area of expertise allows us to serve others in a specific manner that identifies our talent. My mother never passed up an opportunity to share her gift. For anyone who received one of her meals—a neighbor, the pastor, or her family—each one was prepared with love.

There is only one way to do anything, and that is with the spirit of excellence. At the time, I was unaware of the valuable lesson I was learning. I was acquiring an eye for detail. The color of vegetables is critical. A drip on a dinner plate is unacceptable—delicious food should be edible art.

I recently read an article about The Savile Row Company; they are considered Britain's finest tailors. Their attention to detail is their signature feature. This distinguishing quality elevates them above other good tailors and gives them the designation of being the best in their field. They are a great example of how the little things can make a big difference. It's what sets them apart.

No details are insignificant—we must choose those that speak to us and make them components of our signature brand. Success begins with mastering the fine points and this principle transcends education or finances. For starters, we want to know what we do best and model excellence at every opportunity.

> *"If you are going to achieve excellence in big things, you develop the habit in little matters. Excellence is not an exception; it is a prevailing attitude."*

—Colin Powell

TABLE TALK:

List three talents you possess. How does your work in those areas add value to others?

3

FAITH TO MOVE A MOUNTAIN

*"And without faith, it is impossible to please God because
anyone who comes to Him must believe that He exists and
that He rewards those who earnestly seek Him."*

—Hebrews 11:6 NIV

Faith is confidence that it will come to pass.

Everyone loves to hear a speaker present a great story. This belief is evident by the success of TED Talks. We admire a speaker who takes center stage and mesmerizes us with a narrative. Unforgettable stories have a compelling message that grabs our attention. They take us on a journey that inspires, teaches, challenges, or entertains us. But the storyteller aims to make the tale memorable.

Young children also love to hear stories and their favorite narrators are their parents. They want to hear about when their parents were children or any other significant time in their lives. Children hang onto every word as their parents weave a tale of what life was like before they were born. In fact, after several retellings, they interject and supply missing details. As they imagine their mom or dad as children or young adults, a link is formed between the generations. Now they can bear their family history to the next generation.

I was like every other young child. I, too, wanted to hear my parents recite the adventures of their youth. One story I heard a thousand times growing up was the story of the day I was born.

WE ALL HAVE A STORY TO TELL

My parents had been married for several years, and my mother had not conceived. She was thirty and my father forty-three, and they had expected to become pregnant immediately. They experienced the emotional roller-coaster ride infertile couples go through. My parents wanted a child, yet it seemed every couple was pregnant except them. What could be wrong?

After a while, my mother contemplated adoption, but my father would not consider it. Eventually, as the story goes, my Dad relented to my mom's wishes, and they began to explore the adoption process. As God would have it, shortly after that decision, my mother became pregnant with me. Of course, the entire community was excited! Mildred was going to have a baby.

She was ecstatic about becoming a mother. Every day she prayed, thanking God for this miracle, and asking for a healthy baby and a smooth delivery. In her ninth month, during her Bible devotions reading Ezekiel 16:6, she heard in her spirit, "Mark this because you will need it." She marked the verse in her Bible, giving it little thought.

On October 29th, 1951, my mother experienced the first labor contraction. Overwhelmed with excitement and fear, she made her way to the bedroom. Soon she would hold and look into the eyes of the child she prayed for. Mrs. Eunice, her best friend, was summoned. She had five children and was qualified to be a birthing coach. Her words of encouragement would help her friend through the labor pains.

Dr. Penn and his nurse were also notified; they would take charge during those final moments of delivery. These three individuals huddled around my mother as her labor progressed. They shared one goal: a short delivery, a healthy baby, and no complications.

These precious friends and caretakers became a part of my extended family growing up. Mrs. Eunice was one of the ladies at the table, and she and my mother shared birth experiences, recipes, secrets, and the joys and sorrows of life. Dr. Penn was the family physician to everyone in the community. He attended to any medical symptoms my mother could not address.

Unfortunately, my mother had a long, arduous labor. When describing the delivery, she would say in jest, "You took your time getting here."

Finally, I arrived! David and Mildred had a little baby. The news spread through the community; Mildred was doing well and had a healthy baby girl. Her prayers were answered.

Suddenly the atmosphere in the bedroom turned from joy to concern and worry. Dr. Penn's patient was hemorrhaging. He applied pressure to her uterus, but the flow did not stop. Was there time to transport her to the hospital? Would his patient make it? Could he save her?

What do we do when there is a medical crisis and the physician has exhausted all protocols? Does fear overtake us? Do thoughts of dying preempt our thoughts? Will I die having the child I prayed for?

Thankfully, my mother and Mrs. Eunice were women of faith and believed God would intervene. I cannot imagine how empty my life would be if I had lost my mother. These women of simple faith knew God was a healer, and at that moment, my mother remembered the verse she had marked in her Bible.

Now she understood why she heard the prompting, "Mark this because you will need it." She asked Mrs. Eunice to retrieve the family Bible, which was on the table beside her bed, and read Ezekiel 16:6 out loud as she prayed.

The first time nothing happened.

At the second reading, there was still no change.

But at the third reading, Mrs. Eunice read with urgency, and Mildred called out to God.

Then, something shifted.

"Then I passed by and saw you kicking about in your blood, and as you lay there in your blood, I said to you, 'Live!'" (Ezekiel 16:6 NIV).

The flow of blood stopped!

MIRACLES STILL HAPPEN

A mustard seed of faith can move a mountain. My mother's faith opened the door for a miracle—she would live and not die. I smile as I think of her retelling this story. She always ended it with the same declaration. Looking me straight in the eyes, she'd say, "Don't tell me He won't talk to you!" She believes God communicates with those who will listen and obey. There are rewards for obedience. It is a simple yet complex principle by which to live.

How did this act of faith affect me? I had the joy of growing up knowing the love of two parents, and I don't take that for granted. The loss of a parent at a young age can create feelings of rejection or abandonment, which are difficult to overcome. There is a void.

Second, I doubt if my father was equipped to be a successful single parent at the age of forty-four. He was unprepared to cope with a newborn. Most fathers during that era left childcare in the hands of the mother. I probably would have lived with a female relative and experienced some trauma at the loss of both parents. God blessed me to grow up knowing my family loved me. Anything less would be unimaginable. What would my life have been without them? I do not want to picture that scenario.

Finally, I would have missed the opportunity to grow up in a loving community that celebrated my birth and helped raise me. Romans 12:15a reads, "Rejoice with those that rejoice" (NIV). The community rejoiced with my parents when I was born. My mother did not lack a babysitter. Someone was always at her door, ready to take me for a visit to their home. I was a child of the village. Eventually, they nicknamed me "Community Baby," and that name followed me—I believe some people forgot my given name was Carolyn!

How could I not be a believer after hearing this story since I was a small child? Every time I heard it, I said a silent, "Thank You." I am aware of God's intervention and His love. There is a reassurance in knowing He was working and shaping my environment even before I could confess my faith and trust in Him.

My mother gave me unconditional love balanced with structure and order. She had rules and expected me to follow them. My father provided doting attention and helped shape my identity. I knew I was special because that is what he thought. My father's affirmation and love gave me the self-esteem and confidence to enjoy being a female.

The day I was born became one of my mother's miracle stories. Telling them connects the generations and builds emotional and spiritual stamina in those who hear them. Accounts of triumph offer hope to the hearers, instructing them in overcoming adversity and learning to thrive during trials.

The *women at the table* were women of faith, and each of them had their own miracle stories. Success in life required more than wisdom, skill, and ability. They needed God. He has a plan to resolve every challenge. Believe He will give you a miracle story.

> *"And we know that in all things God works*
> *for the good of those who love him,*
> *who have been called according to his purpose."*

—Romans 8:28 NIV

TABLE TALK:

Define faith in your own words and explain what it means to you.

4

THERE IS POWER
IN OUR BELIEFS

With the right attitude, anything is possible.

How do we define wealth? Is it in a bank account balance? Or the number of properties and other goods we own? How do we rate the quality of personal relationships? How important is physical, mental, emotional, and spiritual harmony? Each of us has to answer these questions for ourselves. But we can all agree that wealth is in the eye of the beholder.

As a child, I thought my family was rich—until I became an adult and learned otherwise. Our household income afforded us a comfortable living, but the miners were on strike, or the mines operated on a part-time schedule on occasion. In both scenarios, my father was out of work.

I'm sure those were tough financial times for my family. From my perspective, the state of the economy was insignificant—I was confident my parents would provide whatever we needed for a comfortable existence—an example of naïve childlike faith.

Whether we are an affluent household or live below the poverty level, most homes have a roll of duct tape stored in a drawer. How we use it may be determined by the family's economic status. One of my childhood memories is our duct-taped refrigerator door due to a broken latch.

My father lacked the money to repair it. Did my young mind come to that conclusion? Of course not! I was oblivious because my parents provided all the comforts a child needs to grow up feeling loved. The latch on the refrigerator was not a necessity.

After playing outside, my siblings and I would immediately run to the refrigerator, pull back the duct tape, open the door and select a cold drink or snack. My father scolded us because he would have to re-tape it shut to ensure its contents did not spoil. Unaware of financial lack, my concern was for the goodies inside the fridge. Growing up, we had what we needed, and somehow things we lacked magically appeared. Life was good.

Wealth Is More Than the Money in the Bank

The positive attitudes of my parents shaped my outlook. They were not victims or powerless to control their future. I marvel at my mother's optimism. As a child, I thought she could do anything because she never confessed defeat. When a problem arose, she developed a solution or knew someone who could address the issue.

My father believed hard work could accomplish anything. And work hard, he did. Once, when unemployed, he found two menial jobs: one working on the garbage truck, picking up trash; the other employed as an orderly at the hospital. An uneducated black man, he was determined to provide for his family. An honest job was a means to pay our bills. To his credit, we had a roof over our heads, electricity, and two cars in our driveway. How they managed is beyond me, but with hard work and determination, they did.

They taught and demonstrated their values in practical ways by modeling them. We saw them work hard, show kindness and generosity, and gain respect in the community. Actions speak louder than words. Life was a series of challenges that we could overcome with appropriate solutions.

Therefore, complaining and ungratefulness went unrewarded. During dinner, if my siblings and I grumbled about the meal, my mother would respond, "There are starving children in Africa." I don't know who those children were, but our parents believed they would enjoy the meal without complaining. In other words, we should be thankful for what we had.

To complain means to express dissatisfaction with one's circumstance. It may be less than ideal, but complaining will change nothing—we must find a solution. Our attitude shapes our belief systems, actions, and expectations. Complaining makes everything appear worse and drains us of the necessary motivation and energy to change the situation. This perspective focuses on the problem, not the solution.

A pessimistic outlook is detrimental to our mental and emotional wellbeing. It hinders our ability to build healthy relationships and to develop the resilience required to strive for success in life. According to psychologist Martin Seligman's research, people who see the glass half full live longer, are healthier, enjoy life more, have better social skills, and are more successful in the marketplace.[14] A positive attitude and gratitude have their advantages.

Zig Ziglar said, "Be grateful for what you have and stop complaining—it bores everybody else, does you no good, and doesn't solve any problems."[15] Similarly, Proverbs, the Book of Wisdom for Living, states, "A cheerful heart is good medicine, but a crushed spirit dries up the bones" (Proverbs 17:22 NIV).

Having a positive attitude and practicing gratitude is good medicine and brings life into proper perspective. It creates the mindset of a winner, one who has an "I can do it" spirit and the motivation to overcome any crisis we face.

We can choose to think the best or the worst about our circumstances. It is a daily decision, not once a week or once a year. It takes effort, but a positive outlook optimizes our results. We can choose to be a winner rather than a victim. Every crisis we face has a solution, and we must pursue it with determination. Failure is not an option.

CHOOSING TO BE A WINNER, NOT A VICTIM

Winners refuse to take the easy route. We push through failure and realize that life is a learning process. To succeed, we must continue living our best life. My mother is living proof of this principle. Old age, bad knees, and confinement to a wheelchair do not diminish her enthusiasm for life. Mother does not look nor act her age. In fact, at ninety-five, she purchased new fencing for our family home in West Virginia. At ninety-eight, she had a new tin roof installed. Why tin? Because she always wanted a house with a tin roof. My mother is determined to live until her last breath.

What do we believe about our present circumstances? We can follow her example and live each today to the fullest.

Today, Mother resides in a senior-living apartment building in Columbus, Ohio. Younger residents seek her out to spend time with her. They leave each encounter encouraged and inspired by my mother's wisdom and love. The ability to influence and impact others has no age limit.

Living to the fullest is all about the power of our beliefs. It takes a positive attitude and a grateful spirit to be a winner in life.

"Live your everyday extraordinary!"

—Charles F. Glassman

TABLE TALK:

What are some steps you can take to change or improve your perspective on life?

5

ADVERSITY WILL COME

*Adversity is a roadblock we must navigate successfully,
then continue on the path to greatness.*

I was shocked and devastated. I could not believe what
I was hearing. Carlos, Mrs. Eunice's son, was dead. It
shook our whole community. A cloud of sadness and
heartbreak descended on our neighborhood; young and old
were in disbelief. How could this happen?

Carlos was a strong, athletic teenager with the whole world
ahead of him. He was only a few years older than me, and
his life was cut short. Carlos would be absent from his classmates' high school graduation, would not experience college,
a wedding ceremony, or hearing a child call him daddy. All
his dreams ended that day.

I thought that only older people died. Death came to
those with gray hair, not young people who were healthy and
robust. This tragedy was a paradigm shift, a reality check. We
take life for granted and assume that we will live a long life,
but there are no guarantees.

Mrs. Eunice cried inconsolably as she processed her loss.
The *ladies at the table* were immediately at her side to comfort,
love, and support her. Nothing would turn back the clock,
but they were there when she needed them most. They saw

the pain that consumed her. How would they react to losing a child? They chose not to answer that question.

Taking action, they prepared home-cooked meals, cleaned her house, ran errands, took care of younger children, and encouraged her. Their efforts brought some normalcy to Mrs. Eunice's household, but more compassionate than the chores they performed was their presence. They shared her grief. Watching them, I witnessed friends stepping up and taking charge during a crisis.

RESPONDING TO ADVERSITY

Life is full of joy and sorrow. When we accomplish our goals, we feel exhilarated. We did it! But when we experience a devastating defeat, grief follows. Each woman had experienced a personal tragedy—a miscarriage, a rebellious child, a husband unemployed, poverty, or illness. They were aware that a crisis could make or break them, but amid their challenges, they had hope and acknowledged that life was worth living, so they kept going.

For *the women at the table*, adversity was a prerequisite for perseverance. Perseverance is the character trait acquired by successfully transitioning through a trial. With new insight, we prepare for the next challenge. Life teaches us a valuable lesson: somehow, the challenge I face today can produce a more capable and wiser *me* tomorrow. Plus, I can provide insight and support to someone experiencing similar trauma. I have empathy because I have walked in their shoes.

The ladies expected tomorrow to be a better day because they were steadier and more prudent. They were aware of their limitations, but each of them had developed a personal relationship with God; they were never totally dependent on their friends nor their own abilities. They trusted and relied on God to be their strength in times of trouble. Often we would hear them say, "The Lord will make a way." Those words spoke of their conviction and determination. Their faith would carry them through any crisis.

MOVING TOWARD OUR VICTORY

Tragedy requires our humility, grace, and an unwavering assurance that this, too, will pass. We can expect better days ahead. From *the ladies*, I learned that trials are an aspect of life. Yet, during times of adversity, we must continue moving toward our breakthrough. As we do, our emotional, physical, and spiritual landscapes changes.

From this new vantage point, we have insights we could not comprehend before. These discoveries permit us to perceive better solutions to old problems. We have hope, we see growth, and a new day dawns. Pain subsides, and burdens become light.

The women at the table were courageous—they defied adversity and kept pressing, moving, actively seeking a brighter day. What a valuable lesson to learn—in life, we will experience hardship, but each crisis is an opportunity to develop resilience and courage. Those are the qualities that prepare us for the next life challenge. It's a difficult lesson, but one each of us must learn.

> *"Strength doesn't come from what you can do.*
> *It comes from overcoming the things*
> *you once thought you couldn't."*

—PictureQuotes.com

TABLE TALK:

Describe a close friend or family member's crisis and the impact it had on you.

6

LIFE MUST GO ON

Life is a continuous activity that ultimately reveals the real me.

I saw my mother cry twice. The first time was when Mrs. White falsely accused her of stealing. The second time was December 4th, 1991, a day I will never forget. It was the day my father died.

After forty-three years of marriage, my mother lost her husband, the love of her life, her companion. Her David was gone. There was no hysteria or gut-wrenching wails that emanated from the deep corners of her soul. There was only a look, an expression on her face I had never seen before. Tears streamed from the corners of her eyes, accompanied by a stare that said, *I'm lost. I'm numb. What just happened to me?*

Our mother was grieving, and no words would fill the void of her heart. My siblings and I intertwined our arms around her and held on tight. Mother needed our support, and our grieving would have to wait.

THE LOVE OF A LIFETIME

My father had enjoyed driving my mother to her hair appointments in Beckley, which was forty-five minutes away. For Alpoca residents, going to Beckley was a special treat—we were going to the city. There were shopping malls, restaurants, and the bustling activity of a thriving community.

My mother had her own car, but I suspect my father had another agenda—the excuse to spend time together. A man of few words, his actions spoke for him. The men of his generation took pleasure in driving their wives; it symbolized their role as a leader and protector. After her hair appointment, they had dinner at Bob Evans Restaurant, my father's favorite.

My father desired to make my mother happy, which often resulted in unsolicited gifts. He once traded in her car because she made a favorable comment about another model.

On one occasion, I was home for the holidays and commented on the new kitchen stove. Mother smiled as if she had a secret to share and told me the story of her visit to the furniture store with my dad. She and my dad were at the store, and this stove caught her eye.

Casually, Mother walked over, opened the oven door, stood back to inspect all its features, and gave it an approving look. But she was merely window shopping! She had no desire to purchase it. Several days later, a furniture truck stopped outside our door, and two delivery men unloaded the stove. With smiles on their faces, they announced that her new appliance was here and asked: "Where would you like it?"

My father had secretly purchased the stove because he thought my mother wanted it. This generous provider was her husband, the father of her four children, and the man she loved.

PREPARING FOR THE END

At his eighty-fifth birthday celebration in October 1991, my father was noticeably not himself. He was thinner and less energetic. Not unusual for someone that age. But our family would soon face a crisis.

In November, I received a call from my mother inform-
ing me that my father had been admitted to the hospital for
diagnostic testing. The preliminary prognosis was good, and
with treatment and medication, we assumed he would return
home, and all would be well.

But a month later, I received another call, and this one
crushed me to the core. The test results revealed that my father's
illness was terminal. Our father, our patriarch, the leader of
our family, was dying. Devastated, I could not process what
I was hearing. This disaster could not be! *"Not my father!"*
The person who affirmed me, who thought I was beautiful
because I was his daughter, was fading. He had always made
me feel special.

Growing up, my mother recounted stories of the special
bond my father and I had. He allowed me to tag along as he
ran errands because I cried if he left without me. As a toddler,
I joined him for breakfast and drank my coffee diluted with
water and lots of Carnation canned milk. We had precious
memories of a relationship that began the day I was born.
Soon he would be gone. My heart was heavy with grief.

As my father's hospital stay turned from days to weeks,
it became apparent the inevitable would happen. I had to
acknowledge my father was dying. The doctors determined
there was nothing more they could do, and my father's health
continued to fail. As that day grew closer, my mother stayed
by his bedside, even when the doctors encouraged her to go
home and rest. Exhausted, she finally relented, went home to
take a shower, got some sleep, and returned the following day.

LISTENING FOR THE STILL, SMALL VOICE

Linda, my ex-sister-in-law, picked her up the next morning,
and they returned to the hospital. When my mother walked
into his room and sat in a chair by the bed, she heard a still

small voice in her spirit say, *"Go back and cash the checks!"* She ignored the voice and remained seated. After a few moments, she again heard, *"Go back and cash the checks!"* This time the voice was like thunder. It sounded so loud in one ear that she grabbed it and turned her head in the opposite direction.

Her reaction was noticeable and alarmed Linda, who was sitting beside her. She asked, "What's wrong?" My mother responded, "I need to go back home." Linda was confused. She had spent forty-five minutes driving to the hospital, and now they needed to return home. Without asking any questions, she politely gathered their belongings and returned home.

My father's retirement checks had arrived days earlier and were lying on the kitchen table. Once she got home, my mother gathered them. She and Linda dashed to the bank to make a deposit and returned to the hospital. In life, timing is everything. Within twenty-four hours, my father would die. Any checks not yet deposited would then become non-negotiable. My mother had cashed them in the nick of time. That deposit provided funds needed for living expenses. Now, she could submit documentation verifying herself as my father's beneficiary, but that process takes time. It pays to listen and obey.

My mother has heard the Lord's voice numerous times in her life. Sometimes it was a still, small voice to mark a Bible verse, so quiet and insignificant she could ignore it. Other times it was a loud rumble of thunder that only she could hear, instructing her to deposit checks. How does she explain these spiritual conversations?

Essentially, she believes God is always speaking—it is our responsibility to train our ears to listen. This understanding is an example of her unshakeable faith. I have heard this story many times, and with each hearing, my faith increases. For my mother, God is real: He speaks, gives instructions, and is the source of all wisdom. It's prudent to listen and take action on what we hear.

WE ARE NEVER ALONE

This woman of strength, courage, and faith put her trust in God when my father died. Life can be challenging—it is a journey that consists of twists and turns. However, it is during times of difficulty that our relationship with God is tested and strengthened. Life without her husband would be difficult, but God would comfort her and encourage her—she would never be alone.

> *"Even though I walk through the valley of the shadow of death,*
> *I will fear no evil, for you are with me*
> *your rod and your staff, they comfort me."*

—Psalms 23:4 ESV

TABLE TALK:

What could you do to honor the life of a loved one who has died?

7

OVERCOMING THE
STEREOTYPES

We can become who we want to become. Period!

My hometown zip code contains accurate and inaccurate data about the inhabitants within its boundaries. This information can be an advantage or disadvantage to me. With that information, people make assumptions regarding who I am as an individual, my future earning potential, leadership ability, and even the probability of entering the prison system.

The zip code 90210 for Beverly Hills, California, was the backdrop for a popular TV show by the same name. The show created an image of its young, privileged residents living a glamourous lifestyle. Of course, a zip code doesn't tell the whole story. There are always outliers who refuse to fit the mold and choose to create our own identity. To reach our potential, we must intentionally demolish the preconceived assumptions inherent in a zip code.

I grew up in West Virginia, and for many, a mental image that comes to mind is the *Beverly Hillbillies.* The exact opposite of the *90210* crowd. West Virginia is a section of Appalachia stereotyped as having an uneducated, impoverished, chain-smoking, moonshine-drinking, gun-toting population with a distinctive dialect, easily recognizable by its twang.

Appalachia is more than a geographic area; it's a common culture that is sometimes real and often fictional. This area lags behind the nation economically, and its residents are disproportionately poor, with limited educational opportunities.

In recent years, opioid abuse has plagued the region in epidemic proportions. But the biggest hindrance is its image. When we accept the stereotype, we adopt the limitations inherent within it. West Virginia needs to re-brand its image, which would require its residents to change their self-concept.

The summer I visited my brother in Connecticut, I became aware of the prejudice against West Virginians. Children I met asked me if we wore shoes (even though I was wearing a pair) and ridiculed me when I called a soft drink "pop" and a pair of slacks "britches."

My vocabulary validated their belief that anyone from Appalachia was a hillbilly—uneducated and unsophisticated, even though I was from a middle-class household like many of them. My accent only added to their perception, and I stuck out like a sore thumb.

NOT BELIEVING THE STEREOTYPE

A stereotype is the desire or belief of an individual, society, or culture to box an individual into a preconceived image and never provide access for escape. Perceptions are deceiving and start with judgments about someone we do not know.

For example, if I were from Texas, New York, or Boston, people would make assumptions about who I am based on my accent or dialect. That is unfortunate, but people make decisions and limit our opportunities because of an implicit bias based on speech, mannerisms, where we reside, or some other characteristic.

It is similar to the sketch artist who draws caricatures of individuals. A caricature is an artistic image that over exaggerates or oversimplifies the features of the person being sketched. We do it in fun, and everyone knows not to take the portrait seriously. It is only an image and a poor one; it does not accurately portray the person. There is more to the person than the features that are being exaggerated or simplified.

With a stereotype, we accept what we would dismiss in a caricature. We receive and make assumptions about what we see or hear. And those assumptions are made unconsciously.

In the tenth grade, my teacher, Mrs. Jean Roop, gave me a homework assignment that prepared me to overcome a stereotype. Sitting in my speech class, I wrote down her expectations for the next week. Mrs. Roop told us, "Listen to the nightly news on the three major networks, make notes on the speech patterns and accents of the anchors, and write a report—nothing hard—simply listen and observe."

For the next week on alternate nights, I observed Chet Huntly and David Brinkley on NBC, Peter Jennings on ABC, and Walter Cronkite on CBS. All were respected reporters in the news industry and held the premier position at their respective networks.

My takeaway from watching the anchors was their lack of a regional accent. It was difficult or impossible to tell where they were from, and in fact, they all spoke and sounded the same. Ironically, they had the exact nondescript vocal intonations of my speech teacher.

CREATING OUR OWN IDENTITY

Mrs. Jean Roop was an attractive young brunette who became one of my mentors. She was graceful, stylish, well-spoken, and grew up in Appalachia. She was an excellent teacher who loved her profession and students. The goal of the anchor assignment was to shift our self-image. We would acquire an unrecognizable accent and free ourselves from negative assumptions by the way we spoke.

Mrs. Roop set the bar high, expecting us to emulate national news reporters with years of experience, which was a daunting task. Those anchors never dropped any hint of their regional accent, and her objective was for her students to rebrand themselves and create a new identity through this assignment.

For the next three years, her classes helped prepare other students and me to become model speakers and outgrow our *hillbilly* dialect. Regional colloquialisms were out, and pronunciation corrected, she pushed us outside the stereotype; and slowly, we began to envision ourselves refusing to carry the additional weight of a stereotype.

This exercise had many benefits. It encouraged me to step outside my surroundings' cultural limitations and realize my birthplace was secondary; it was my beginning, not my end. What I carried, what was inside of me—my strengths and abilities—were tools of destiny. A zip code would not define me. Life consists of breaking through barriers that others create for us and breaking out of those we voluntarily make.

I reaped long-term benefits from this assignment throughout my life. It was a lesson resulting in transformation. When I graduated from high school and went to college, I often heard, "You don't sound like you're from West Virginia." And I know for a fact that Mrs. Roop would be proud of me.

Never lose sight of what you are destined to accomplish.

TABLE TALK:

What stereotypes have you resisted and refused to embrace?

PART FOUR
CONCLUSION
MAXIMIZING THE MOMENT!

To love is to act in the long-term best interest of another.

—Father Ed, quoted by Casey Crawford

What happens when we put others first? We become transformational influencers and change the world. When we intentionally act in others' best interests, we increase our ability to make a difference in people's lives.

Each of us has a voice, a message, and the ability to provide hope and encouragement. We can make someone's day by sharing our skills and talents and serving them. It's a simple yet effective formula for living our best life.

Show up strong and let them see who you are!

1

A COMMUNITY IS A VILLAGE WHERE LOVE ABOUNDS

"Love must be the prime mover for everything we do."

—Eric L. Warren

What moves a diverse group of people to intertwine their lives and become a village that provides for each member? How do we transition from self-centered thinking to caring for the larger community? How do we value and pursue our own goals to integrate and appreciate the abilities of others?

How is the concept of community demonstrated in the lives of individuals? According to anthropologist Margaret Mead, social and cultural development in a people group develops when its members value each member within the group. They recognize that every person is worthy of love, care, and protection. There is an awareness that everyone can contribute to the welfare of the community.

For an anthropologist, there must be some physical evidence that the group has made this transition. Mead states that an ideal example is a healed human femur discovered in an archaeological dig. Yes, she said a "healed human femur."[16]

What does this artifact say about civilized people? It means someone cared enough about the injured person to love, feed, and nurse them back to health. Another person considered them a valuable member of the group. This behavior is an example of love in action.

A powerful lesson to be learned is—we are stronger as a team than individuals. When individuals unite around a shared vision to function in their areas of expertise, they position the group to succeed. This unity allows each person to fulfill their mission and contribute to the success of the community. Both the individual and group accomplish their goals as working together builds a synergistic relationship between the community and individual members.

When we look beyond ourselves and intentionally serve others, our lives become significant. Then we discover our purpose—our reason for living. In the process, we become our best selves, learn from adversity, and live by values that benefit others.

The *women at the table* were a group of nurturers. More than neighbors, they were individuals who appreciated one another—using Margaret Mead's analogy, individuals who allowed broken femurs to heal. Their small community modeled what it meant to care for others as they cared for themselves.

VILLAGE LIFE

All the men in the neighborhood worked for the Slab Fork Coal Company. If the wives worked outside the home, they did day work, cleaning the homes of white families in the surrounding communities. The village shared mutual employment, culture, church experience, and country life's ups and downs. They were indeed a village of people supporting one another and helping each other rear children.

Each child was a child of the village, and any adult could correct, spank, tell us to go home, or encourage us, as needed. It was an unspoken rule that everyone knew and respected. Adults felt a sense of responsibility for the children in their neighborhoods and functioned as surrogate parents. This was a community where everyone knew everyone else and looked out for their neighbors.

This community welcomed my parents and supported them and their children. My mother was a gracious hostess who welcomed everyone to her table and nourished each guest's body, soul, and spirit. Love was the prime motivator for everything she did.

My parent's neighbors on the left were Eunice and Ed Logwood. The Logwoods were the parents of five children, with one on the way when my parents became their neighbors. Mrs. Eunice was a young mother who soon began to rely on my mother to assist her growing family. My mother taught her young neighbor how to cook and manage her household and even attended her children's births. An attentive student, Mrs. Eunice eventually became an excellent cook and housekeeper.

The neighbors on the right were Ruth and Goalie Martin, who became my parents' closest friends. Mr. Goalie worked at the mine, and Mrs. Ruth was a stay-at-home wife. They had no children but were surrogate parents to one niece. The Martins and my parents visited one another's homes for social get-togethers and even took day trips to visit friends.

Helen and John Pennix lived several houses down from my parents and had five children. They were both active in the Mt. Olivet Baptist Church, which everyone attended. Mr. John was a deacon and Sunday School superintendent. Mrs. Helen was the Sunday School teacher.

Janie and George Scott, with their six children, lived several houses down from my parents. The Scotts were an unconventional couple who adhered to a different set of rules. We seldom saw them together, as they appeared to live separate lives in the same house. They did not attend church, and the familial structure observed in other homes was absent. However, it worked for them. Even with their eccentric lifestyle, they were accepted and welcomed in the community.

THE WOMEN AT THE TABLE: WOMEN UNITED

In this neighborhood, my mother learned to love women who eventually sat at her kitchen table. Mrs. Ruth Martin, Mrs. Eunice Logwood, Mrs. Helen Pennix, and Mrs. Janie Scott became her friends and formed a sisterhood that lasted a lifetime.

These are *the women at the table*. Each of them created a memory, a place in time full of wisdom that taught, corrected, challenged, and empowered me to be a better person. Each offered a unique experience and a measure of grace that produced the person called Carolyn Cross Warren. I proudly stand on their shoulders.

They were strong, beautiful, elegant, graceful, loving, wise, patient, giving, and kind. Women of vision, leaders who were unconcerned with titles, aimed to use their boundless energy and talents to serve. They were mentors and influencers before it was fashionable. These are the women who, with a smile and open arms, invited me to sit at their table. To each of them, I say, "thank you!"

> *"Two roads diverged in a wood, and I—*
> *I took the one less traveled by,*
> *And that has made all the difference."*

—Robert Frost, "The Road Not Taken."

2

PAYING IT FORWARD

Forward is intentional action that moves us
toward our desired future.

ORDINARY PEOPLE MAKING
EXTRAORDINARY IMPACT

I like to start my day drinking a Starbucks hazelnut caramel macchiato extra hot with an extra shot. One morning as I was going through the local Starbucks drive-through, I told the barista I wanted to pay for the car behind me. I decided to take part in the Starbucks "pay it forward" challenge taking place nationally. No one asked me to participate, but I wanted to bring joy to someone and hopefully inspire them to do the same.

We can design random acts of kindness or benevolent challenges to address specific needs or solve problems. Recently there was the "ice bucket" challenge where participants dumped a bucket of ice water on their heads to raise funds for ALS. As another example, Secret Santas pay the balance on toy layaways at local stores before Christmas.

The journalist Tom Llamas, who reports for the Nightly ABC News, did a segment on the Breakfast Santas outside Dayton, Ohio.[17] This group of individuals has a straightforward mission: encourage someone and make their Christmas brighter and full of joy.

On one occasion, about fifteen people arrived at a Bob Evans restaurant and paid for their meal by giving the two waitresses a brown paper bag filled with money for their bill, tipping fourteen hundred extra.

These are all examples of ordinary people who want to make an extraordinary impact on someone's life. However, we don't need a challenge to perform acts of kindness that have a tremendous effect.

WE CARRY ANSWERS

Each of us was created to work toward results that net positive outcomes. With traits as unique and distinctive as our fingerprints, we each carry the answer to some problem or possess the ability to improve someone's life. Our strengths or gifts are the answers others are waiting to receive. A Harvard degree is not necessary, nor the C-suite of a major corporation or millions in our bank accounts. The only requirement is understanding what we carry.

> DO YOU UNDERSTAND WHAT MAKES YOU UNIQUE?

We become powerful when we can answer that question. That knowledge will prepare us to make a difference in others' lives.

IDENTIFYING WHO NEEDS ME

The next step is to seek to serve others selflessly. It is in giving that we change lives and make our own meaningful. We can designate every day to give away what we possess. There is no need to wait or limit ourselves to a volunteer initiative or the annual United Way campaign; we can do great things every single day. Identify someone and create a moment that changes his or her life.

GIVING

Finally, we can give with no thought to what we will receive in return. It is not about us; it's our legacy—the lasting memory we leave behind. Memories are potent images that impact us on different levels. When we change someone's life, creating a moment filled with possibility, we sear that image and moment into their heart and mind.

Memory is the faculty by which we retain impressions and information, consciously or unconsciously, and subsequently, recall.[18] We recall an image each time we share our encounter. We relive the event and develop a more profound mental and emotional impression with each retelling. We also carry that memory which reinforces our ability to influence others. Each of us has the power to change multiple lives with one simple act.

FINDING OUR ZONE OF GENIUS

Ebony, my oldest daughter, often says I am the only person she knows who will pay a service provider and then offer free advice about their business or coach them on a personal issue.

For example, I might share with a service provider how they can market their business or the importance of developing a business plan. While I am in the stylist's chair, I might conduct a personal development coaching session. Then once my service is complete, I pay their fee, plus a twenty percent tip.

My goal is to move the needle for them while we are together. One of my *zones of genius* is the ability to listen and formulate strategies or solve problems to allow them to grow their business. These informal meetings are my way of supporting their vision, and hopefully, creating moments of opportunity that will change their lives.

I am reminded of *the women at the table* who paid it forward by investing in me. They used an informal setting without fanfare and filled that time with significant growth. These ladies never knew their impact on me because I had yet to realize or value these encounters. But those ordinary, sometimes insignificant moments created extraordinary potential in my life. This book is my attempt to acknowledge and celebrate them for what they shared.

THE CHALLENGE

I challenge us all to intentionally create opportunities that equip and empower those we meet. What does the world need from us? They need us! Let's visualize ourselves as walking empowerment zones filled to the brim with resources, knowledge, and solutions—on a mission to ignite exponential growth in other people. Our uniqueness has equipped each of us to solve others' problems and become a new chapter in their life story. We have something to give, and someone is waiting for us!

> *"Every individual matters.*
> *Every individual has a role to play.*
> *Every Individual makes a difference."*
>
> —Jane Goodall

3

IT DOESN'T TAKE MUCH TO CHANGE A LIFE

The gift of time is the greatest gift of all.

One of my superpowers is the ability to make people feel important. One way I demonstrate this is by giving my undivided attention while conversing with them. I believe there is a reason our paths crossed at this very moment, and I need to engage them in a way that adds value to their lives. I zoom in on them and block out everyone else because *we* may never have this moment again.

ELEVATING EVERY INTERACTION

What if we elevated every interaction, from a casual encounter to an intentional exchange, to add value to the person we are meeting? We have the power to make every interaction memorable and full of learning, positioning them for success.

In business circles, we hear the importance of making a great first impression. It increases our ability to receive every benefit the interaction has to offer. We usually focus on how the meeting can help us and not the person we are meeting.

Let's shift our focus and give new friends our full attention. What would happen if every encounter became an opportunity to engage on a deeper level, a quest to identify their unique skills—and doing so authentically? We could make better first impressions by adding to their lives and helping them gain greater insight into their skills.

WHEN WE LOOK FOR TREASURE, WE MAY FIND IT

How might we do this? By intentionally looking for ways to encourage others, show compassion, actively listen, share knowledge, or simply express appreciation for the talents and abilities they have. Looking for the best in others can be a game-changer—it's a simple action but can change our relationship's trajectory and focus.

We can give compliments that pinpoint and identify areas of expertise. What a powerful tool to empower others! We become known as motivators, encouragers, and influencers. This perception opens the door to trust and respect from those with whom we engage.

180 SECONDS IS ALL IT TAKES

I call this process my *three-minute rule*. The goal is to engage fully for a minimum of three minutes. If I need to move on, I'll ask someone I'm speaking with to accompany me to my next meeting, extending our time together. I'll grab the person's hand to signal that they are important and to ensure we keep pace while we progress. I am choosing to include them in my life. I don't miss this moment.

A lot can happen in three minutes. If I have more time to listen, that's even better. Growth can occur when the goal is to help someone else. Choosing to be selfless, valuing others, and creating a moment for someone tells them they matter. We give them our time, communicating that they are seen and heard. Unfortunately, most individuals will never have such an encounter, but we can change that! We can make an unforgettable first impression and people will remember us. *The women at the table* provided numerous opportunities for me by giving of their time, grabbing my hand, and allowing me to walk with them.

If we move beyond "me" thinking, we can connect with others and contribute to their lives. We are not empty vessels, but people overflowing with abilities. Every day, we need an outlet to continue growing. The three-minute rule is a great way to make an excellent first impression and live a life that matters. We can turn every ordinary conversation into an extraordinary living experience.

It's time to give someone at least three minutes of our day! Let's grab someone's hand so they can take the journey with us.

"Everybody has the power to change other people's lives."

—Richard Curtis, founder of the Comic Relief charity

*"You are where you are today because you
stand on somebody's shoulders.
And wherever you are heading,
you cannot get there by yourself.
If you stand on the shoulders of others, you have a reciprocal
Responsibility to live your life so that others may stand on
your shoulders.
It's the quid pro quo of life.
We exist temporarily through what we take,
But we live forever through what we give."*

—Vernon Jordan

ACKNOWLEDGMENTS

I am grateful to the members of *the village* who loved, supported, and believed in me as I grew up. Without their contributions, this book would not be possible. My deepest thanks go to my mother and father, Mildred and David Cross, who prayed for a child and loved me unconditionally. I am humbled by your love.

This book would have been no more than an idea had it not been for Johari Mitchell, Chiquita Toure, and my daughter Monica Warren. These women are all great writers, and they helped me take what was a simple life story and give it structure.

As I brainstormed with them, they listened, provided encouragement, and helped me tell my story. My friends and daughter were honest with their critiques, and with each revision, they patiently reread the manuscript. Thank you for gifting me with your precious time. I've always said I have thick skin, and you made me prove it!

To Lisa Marie Pepe and Pam Brossman, thank you. Your workshops were a vital part of my online journey.

To my Equippers City Church family and specifically the women I coached, taught, and had fun with, I am grateful. You believed in me and allowed me to share your lives.

To my daughters Ebony, Charisse, and Monica, you have been my biggest fans. You are more than daughters—I consider you my friends. It's incredible how mother-daughter relationships evolve. I respect you and love you for knowing who you are, intentionally sharing your lives with others, and making a difference in the world. I am proud of you.

Lonnell Johnson, my brother-in-law, thank you for pushing and encouraging me to the finish line when I began to think no one was interested in this story.

And finally, I want to thank my amazing husband, Eric Warren. He is my best friend, my confidant, the person I enjoy spending time with, and the one who has modeled how a relationship with the Lord looks. Eric, you are the love of my life. Thank you for your support and for always making me smile.

NOTES

Part One: Preparing for Success

[1] "20 Favorite Jewish Quotes," Feb 22, 2014, https://www.aish.com.

[2] James Strong, *The New Strong's Exhaustive Concordance of the Bible,* Comfort Print Edition (Nashville: Thomas Nelson, Inc., 1995), 1439.

[3] John C. Maxwell, *The 15 Invaluable Laws of Growth, Live Them and Reach Your Potential* (New York: Hachette Book Group, 2012), 20.

[4] Malcolm Gladwell, *Outliers: The Story of Success* (New York: Little, Brown and Company, 2008), 37-42, 45, 55, 128, 144.

[5] "Here's Why Manners and Etiquette are Important for Your Success," accessed June 4, 2020, https://socialmettle.com.

[6] Lexicon Publication, Inc. *Etiquette, The New Lexicon Webster's Dictionary of the English Language,* 1990 Edition (New York: Lexicon Publications, Inc., 1990), 325.

[7] Random House, Inc., *The Random House Book of Etiquette,* Volume 1, 2nd Printing (New York: Random House, 1967), Introduction.

[8] "*7 Incisive Clarence Thomas Quotes From 25 Years in Office,* July 1, 2016, https://thefederalist.com.

Part Two: Choosing Our Values

[9]   Dr. Frank Crane Quotes: https://www.inspirationalstories. com/quotes/dr-frank-crane-the-golden-rule-is-of-no-use/.

[10] "Nelson Mandela Quotes," accessed May 10, 2020, https:// www.brainyquoted.com.

[11] "Maya Angelou Quote," accessed May 10, 2020, https:// www.goodreads.com/quotes/7273813-do-the-bes t-you-can-until-you-know-better-then_

Part Three: Believing It's Possible

[12] "What Are Newton's Laws of Motion?" Accessed February 20, 2021, https://www.thoughtco.com/ what-are-newtons-laws-of-motion.

[13] Paul G. Stoltz, "The Adversity Advantage Quotes," https:// www.goodreads.com/work/quotes/1315386-the-adversity-a dvantage-turning-everyday-struggles-into-everyday-greatn.

[14] Why Your Glass is Actually Half Full—The Value of Positive Psychology." Accessed May 20, 2020, https://www. listeningpartnership.com/insight.

[15] Zig Ziglar Quotes," accessed February 16, 2020, https:// www.brainyquote.com.

Part Four: Conclusion—Maximizing the Moment!

[16] "An Anthropologist Explains the First Sign of Civilization" Accessed April 8, 2021, https://doerlife.com/ an-anthropologist-explains-the-first-sign-of-civilization/.

[17] "America Strong: Waitresses receive $1,400 tip from charitable group, December 15, 2019," Accessed May 15, 2020, https://abcnews.go.com.

[18] Lexicon Publication, Inc. "Memory." *The New Lexicon Webster's Dictionary of the English Language,* 1990 Edition (New York: Lexicon Publications, Inc., 1990), 623.

YOUR NEXT STEPS WITH
CAROLYN A. WARREN
and
THE WOMEN AT THE TABLE

Join the *WOMEN AT THE TABLE* community to continue the conversations that will empower you to show up boldly to make a difference.

   ✓ Join the *Women at the Table* email list and receive content to continue your growth journey.

Go to www.carolynawarren.com and enter your details.

Go to *The Women at the Table*: *The Book* Group, on Facebook and request to join.

   ✓ You'll get instant access to bonus material and additional training that will equip you to make a difference. We'll also discuss how to apply the information in the book to your life.

   ✓ Plan to attend the annual *The Women at the Table* conference. You are empowered to take a seat at the table and become an influencer. Join other women who share your vision and dream to make an impact. This is your chance to become motivated and inspired and to learn new strategies to bring out the best in the people you meet.

Go to www.carolynawarren.com

ABOUT THE AUTHOR

CAROLYN A. WARREN is a speaker, trainer, and leadership coach who has trained and mentored women for more than thirty years. As a John Maxwell Team member and a behavior analysis (DISC) trainer she encourages women to embrace their gifts, move beyond their fears and intentionally make a difference in the world. Carolyn lives in Charlotte, North Carolina, with her husband Eric.

CPSIA information can be obtained
at www.ICGtesting.com
Printed in the USA
LVHW090343020921
696759LV00008B/52